PENGUIN BOOKS

POP CULTURE

Christopher Healy has written for publications including *Salon*, *Cookie*, *The Washington Post*, *Child*, *Cargo*, *Glamour*, and *Real Simple*. Despite his daughter's conviction that "Daddy's job is writing about me," many of his articles and essays have actually focused on other topics. He lives with his wife and daughter in Brooklyn.

THE SANE MAN'S GUIDE TO THE INSANE
WORLD OF NEW FATHERHOOD

Christopher Healy

PENGUIN BOOKS

PENGUIN BOOKS

Published by the Penguin Group

Penguin Group (USA) Inc., 375 Hudson Street, New York,
New York 10014, U.S.A.

Penguin Group (Canada), 90 Eglinton Avenue East, Suite 700, Toronto,
Ontario, Canada M4P 2Y3 (a division of Pearson Penguin Canada Inc.)

Penguin Books Ltd, 80 Strand, London WC2R 0RL, England

Penguin Ireland, 25 St Stephen's Green, Dublin 2, Ireland
(a division of Penguin Books Ltd)

Penguin Group (Australia), 250 Camberwell Road, Camberwell, Victoria 3124,
Australia (a division of Pearson Australia Group Pty Ltd)

Penguin Books India Pvt Ltd, 11 Community Centre, Panchsheel Park,
New Delhi - 110 017, India

Penguin Group (NZ), cnr Airborne and Rosedale Roads, Albany,
Auckland 1310, New Zealand (a division of Pearson New Zealand Ltd)

Penguin Books (South Africa) (Pty) Ltd, 24 Sturdee Avenue, Rosebank,
Johannesburg 2196, South Africa

Penguin Books Ltd, Registered Offices:
80 Strand, London WC2R 0RL, England

First published in Penguin Books 2006

10 9 8 7 6 5 4 3 2 1

Copyright © Christopher Healy, 2006
All rights reserved

Portions of Chapter 12 appeared in different form on Salon.com.

LIBRARY OF CONGRESS CATALOGING-IN-PUBLICATION DATA

Healy, Christopher.
Pop culture : the sane man's guide to the insane world of new fatherhood /
by Christopher Healy.
    p.   cm.
ISBN   0-14-303716-1
1. Fatherhood. I. Title.

HQ756.H384 2006
649'.10242—dc22   2005055537

Printed in the United States of America
Set in Melior with Frutiger
Designed by Daniel Lagin

For Bryn and Noelle, my muses

CONTENTS

Not Your Father's Fatherhood

Thirty years ago

A man wakes up early one Saturday morning and, braving possible milk spillage or accidental inhalation of pink cereal dust, doles out bowls of Franken Berry to his children all by himself, thereby allowing his wife to sleep in until 8 a.m.: Phone calls to the Father of the Year parade committee ensue.

Today

A young father reads bilingual board books to the infant straddling his chest in a Baby Björn, carries chilled bottles of prepumped breast milk in his over-the-shoulder "dad bag," and pores over the nutritional info on Zwieback boxes with the precision of a C.S.I. agent: He is roundly scolded for not giving the milk to his infant in a natural-shaped, bubble-reducing bottle with an orthodontically correct nipple.

Hello, men. Welcome to fatherhood in the age of mixed messages.

If you work long, exhausting hours to ensure financial stability for your family, someone will accuse you of neglecting your child; if you quit your job to stay home with your baby, someone will tell you you're not being a proper provider. If you place your kid in a small, family day care, someone will warn you he's not getting enough preparation for the mental rigors of kindergarten; if you enroll him in an elite preschool that instructs two-year-olds in Linux programming, someone will tut-tut you for rushing him into adulthood. If you buy your daughter jars of organic baby food, someone will say you're wasting money by not purchasing Gerber in bulk—and someone *else* will say you're wasting money by not pulping your own yams with a mortar and pestle.

To stay sane, you must learn to live among both the people who expect too little from you and those who expect too much.

For most of our own fathers, being "involved" didn't mean much more than attending the random soccer game or maybe explaining to us why we were being sent to our rooms. And there are plenty of guys who still play that way. Even if you're the type of modern dad who doesn't shudder at the thought of changing a diaper, many people will reflexively assume you're one of those I'm-just-here-to-bring-home-the-bacon-and-teach-the-boys-how-to-throw-a-tight-spiral dads. These folks will either heap kudos upon you simply for being present or insult your intelligence by reminding you that your infant should not leave the house naked in a snowstorm.

Frustrating you in an altogether different way will be the increasingly influential hyperparents, the anxiety worshippers who believe that you exist to serve your offspring. Their pathological overthinking of all things child-related has led to the Mom-on-the-Brink becoming a pop-culture icon (whether in the farce of *Desperate Housewives* or the unwashed naturalism of reality shows in which wives are swapped and imported nannies rule). Over-the-top competitiveness and unreasonable, ever-shifting standards of parental excellence are driving mothers mad (and spawning a spate of backlash books like Judith Warner's *Perfect Madness* and Susan

Douglas and Meredith Michaels's *The Mommy Myth*). And fathers—no matter how easygoing and casual they think themselves to be—are being affected, too; they'd *have* to be. Who stands in the middle of a hurricane and says, "*Pffft,* I don't mind getting a little wet"?

So here we are at a time in history when it is extraordinarily difficult to be deemed a "good parent," yet more and more guys are voluntarily signing up for active dad duty. We are part of a new generation of fathers who—whether it's due to a more progressive belief system, a genuine desire to have a greater impact on the lives of our children, simple male ego, or some mix of the three—have decided to wear our mashed banana stains like battle scars ("Burp cloths? We don't need no stinkin' burp cloths"). One out of every five preschoolers with a working mom is cared for primarily by his father, and almost half of all Gen-X dads—including those who work—spend three to six hours a day on domesticity (only 39 percent of baby-boomer fathers devoted as much of their schedule to their kids). Today's situation may be far from any kind of coparenting ideal, but we're not stuck back in *The Donna Reed Show* either.

Having made the conscious decision to be involved fathers, many guys are also seeking to bone up on the parenting process long before their wives[1] give birth (the Internet and a proliferation of child-care manuals make this pretty easy nowadays). I did the same thing. But one crucial piece of information that was never revealed to me in the prenatal period was that upon entering fatherhood, I

---

1. This book is for all dads. That includes not only those men in traditional married heterosexual couples, but single dads, divorced dads, gay dads, cohabitating but unmarried dads, nonbiological dads, or any combination of the above. However, the text would get tiresome rather quickly if I were to repeatedly spell out the correct terminology for each of these possibilities. So you will frequently see me make reference to your "wife." Should you not have a wife, please feel free to mentally substitute "mother of your child," "partner," "lover," "soul mate," "betrothed," "ex," "old lady," "odalisque," "best friend with benefits," or whatever other term would more appropriately apply to your situation.

would find myself suddenly immersed in a whole new culture—one with its own laws, lingo, and etiquette. The technical aspects of being a dad (e.g., preparing bottles, dispensing medicine from droppers, figuring out the right way to hold the baby) were the simple parts. It was feeling my way through the labyrinth of playgroup politics, overpriced child-goods stores, and finger-pointing news articles that made me want to throw open my window and treat innocent passersby to a *Network*-style screaming fit.

I was suddenly stranded in a new world. I needed a knowledgeable guide, a Sherpa Dad. I wanted someone to answer the really pressing questions that pop up once you become a father: How do I protect my daughter from our friends' obnoxious kids? How long should I wear a hair shirt if I let her sit through two straight hours of *Dora the Explorer*? Who decided that people under five will only listen to trilly folk music?

From the people you run into (former friends who will begin an all-out war with you over the merits of sharing a bed with their son until he makes the honor roll) to the changes in your surroundings (bookshelves that held titles by Nick Hornby and Michael Chabon slowly begin to sag under the weight of the works of H. A. Rey and Margaret Wise Brown), you will be rapidly immersed in a new culture that can sometimes be illogical or downright bizarre.

In my own case, as time went by, I realized that my only reliable sources of information on these all-important issues were other dads. We'd encounter one another at parents groups, by swing sets in the park, in the baby-food aisle at the grocery store, during pickup time at day care. Each of our brief exchanges was a chance to compare notes, to either openly ask a question or at least subtly draw out information about the other guy's kid, spouse, or home. In a best-case scenario, the data we'd glean would provide us with a solid answer to some question that had been nagging us for weeks. Or at the very least, we'd walk away knowing that whatever had been worrying or frustrating us was not unique.

There's no more comforting feeling than hearing another dad say, "Yes, I also find that having Buzz Lightyear on my son's diapers is just goading him to pull his pants down," or "No, it's not just you—I will also allow strawberry stains to set in on the sofa cushions because I can't be bothered to undo the safety locks on the cleaning-supply cabinet." Sometimes just knowing you're not alone is enough to make you feel better the next time you catch yourself singing the *Bob the Builder* theme song when your child's not even in the room.

I make no claims of being an expert or of having all the answers. But I do have a child—my daughter, Bryn, who is now four years old. And I've spent a year probing the minds of more than a hundred other fathers and fathers-to-be from all around the country (and beyond!).[2] These exchanges with my brethren served two purposes: They confirmed for me that each of my sometimes unconventional thoughts on fatherhood was shared by at least one other guy out there; and they enlightened me to a number of topics that I hadn't even considered (like the common practice of covertly removing batteries out of your kid's electronic noisemakers).

As a guide to parenting, this book is certainly not complete. There are hundreds of other writers out there who can fill you in on the details of eliminating cradle cap or installing protective door-knob covers. My intention is to introduce you to some of the major issues orbiting the culture of fatherhood today, and, since men don't

---

2. For the record, the appearance of any dad's name or words within the pages of this book in no way indicates that the dad in question agrees with all the opinions expressed by me, the author. (Does that sound legal enough?)

talk to one another enough about being a dad (or anything important, for that matter), to stir you guys into kicking up some man-to-man dialogue on these topics.

Also, this book is not for everybody. I am writing all this based on the assumption that, since you are reading this, you at least *intend* to be an active part of your child's life (I'm either an optimist or a prick, you decide). My sampling of fathers, while by no means scientific, included Democrats and Republicans, preachers and atheists, ice climbers and librarians, construction workers and webmasters, all of whom are supremely devoted parents, incredibly active in their children's lives. So whoever you are out there, you're not alone; some other guy is also wondering how he's supposed to adjust his life in order to add Involved Dad to his résumé.

So read on and check out what I (and the other guys) have to say. Why not? At worst, you'll come to the conclusion that I'm a terrible parent with awful advice—which can prove to be an awesome self-esteem boost for you (nothing will pump up confidence in your own parenting skills like coming across someone who is embarrassingly bad at the job). But if I succeed in my mission here, none of you will ever second-guess your choice of high chair just because a woman at Babies "R" Us shook her head as you picked up a model that she obviously considered subpar. And you won't consider relocating to a cabin in the Black Hills after the first time one of your single, childless friends mocks the fact that you want to be home by 7 p.m. And when your wife hits you with the impossible-to-answer question of "Did the baby miss me?" you'll just say . . . well, actually, if you figure out a good response to that one, maybe you can write and let me know.

POPCULTURE

PART I

PREGNANCY: THE MANDATORY WAITING PERIOD

There is no wormhole to fatherhood. You won't be lounging about one day in your regular childless world when suddenly—bamf!—you're instantly teleported to an alternate reality where the longneck microbrew in your hand has morphed into a bottle of soy formula and the Esquire you were reading has been mysteriously replaced by The Poky Little Puppy.

No, the culture of fatherhood will begin to slowly seep into your life, little by little, the same way cantaloupe invades a fruit salad, its juice gradually overwhelming all the banana bits, grape halves, and kiwi slices until everything in the bowl just tastes like melon. Thankfully, the slowness of the process allows the father-to-be several months (about nine, give or take) of buffer zone during which he can begin to familiarize himself with the strange ways of his new world, before the birth of his child forces him, rather unceremoniously, into total immersion. This adjustment period is known as The Pregnancy.

CHAPTER 1

The First Trimester

READY OR NOT: Finding Out and What Comes After

"My wife came out of the bathroom and I knew. She didn't say anything, she wasn't waving the stick; she just had this look on her face and I knew."   —George R., Austin, TX

The road to fatherhood begins with the words, "We're having a baby." Or perhaps, "I'm pregnant," "Guess who's going to be a daddy?" or "Turns out it wasn't the clams that made me sick yesterday." And whether those words are whispered in your ear, shouted over the phone, or written on a cake, most men feel that their life is altered from that moment on. I certainly did.

My wife had called me at work with what was, in retrospect, a strangely urgent request to come home on time so we could go out for dinner. Of course, I suspected nothing. It had been only a week since we'd begun trying to get pregnant, so the possibility that we might have gotten sperm and egg to meet already had not yet entered my mind. I just figured that my wife, a writer herself who had been working from home, was getting a little stir-crazy.

When I got home she was lounging on the living room sofa, staring off into space. "You're that bored, huh?" I asked.

"Oh yeah, it's been a really dull day," she replied coolly. "I worked all morning, went out to grab a sandwich for lunch, stopped at the drugstore on the way back, found out I'm pregnant, and the rest of the afternoon's been pretty much just waiting for you to come home."

Damn, she was good! She didn't even end on the word "pregnant"; she kept right on going. My wife tells me she'll never forget the expression on my face (a cross between an excited Ralphie finally getting his Red Ryder BB gun in *A Christmas Story* and a startled Buckwheat brushing into a haunted-house skeleton). I asked her if she was serious three or four times before I finally threw my arms around her, wept, and began bouncing like I was trying to stay balanced on an invisible pogo stick.

"I was returning home from work and decided to stop at Men's Warehouse to shop for a couple of dress shirts. My wife called while I was shopping to let me know the test was positive. So I rushed out of that store and into Borders across the street, picked up a couple of pregnancy and fatherhood books, and sped home." —Brian B., Las Vegas, NV

So there I was, a father-to-be for all of thirty seconds, and already I was acting like a complete freak. That's partly what made me believe I had begun some kind of metamorphosis into a completely different person.

From that point on, everything I read and everybody I talked to made me believe that parenthood would be so fulfilling, so soul-nourishing that I would become 100 percent child-focused, with no room left—or desire for—anything else. Now, you see, I had nurtured a whole lot of *non*-baby-related interests over the previous twenty-nine years, so I supposed they would have to get erased somehow, à la *Men in Black*. Could the appearance of an infant trigger some sort of psychological switch that would cut off any desire for thought-provoking literature, stimulating conversation, restaurants with fabric tablecloths, or repeated viewings of *Airplane!*?

As it would turn out, no. But I was going to discover that soon enough.

> "Finding out I was going to be a dad was exciting, but it also made me so nervous I thought I might throw up—like when you're about to speak in front of a large group of people. I take a lot of cues from my wife, though, and she seemed so confident that the whole thing seemed normal very quickly. In other words, it was weird how *un*weird it felt."
>
> —Jeff R., Chicago, IL

MOODY BLUES: You vs. Your Wife's Hormones

Thanks to years of film and television viewing, you may enter the first trimester thinking, "Okay, this is the part where she threatens to beat me with a broom if I don't run out and find her a pint of Chunky Monkey at midnight." However, mood swings (i.e., your wife transforms from mild-mannered Everywoman to emotional powder keg) and bizarre food cravings are not just Hollywood myths (my wife developed a sudden affinity for egg noodles).

Moods change rapidly and without warning, so while your wife is with child, even seemingly innocuous discussions need to be handled delicately. Example: Over dinner, you and she are laughing through a jovial conversation about all the names you wouldn't choose for your child because they rhyme with diseases, when suddenly—in a jarring tone shift that, if your life were a film, would be accompanied by the screech of a turntable needle being yanked across a spinning LP—your wife starts screaming at you because you accidentally mentioned the name of her dead Aunt Lydia.

In order to steer through this maelstrom of emotions, you may be called upon to exercise a superhuman level of understanding and empathy. Always keep in mind that the mom-to-be's outbursts are estrogen-induced, involuntary, and may often be followed by an apology from her—unless, of course, you spitefully take her to task for every minor snap. Just remind yourself of that tequila bender back in junior year; you wouldn't want to be held accountable for the things you did and said that night, would you?

Morning sickness, that other iconic symptom of pregnancy, may contribute to the crankiness. It's hard *not* to feel sympathetic toward someone suffering from regular stomach heavings, but morning sickness is not always a visible condition. So if you see a spike in the frequency and intensity of your wife's crabby streaks, recurring nausea might be the culprit—even if there's no projectile vomiting to assure you of that fact.

"My wife felt sick quite often, but she threw up just once," said Kevin K., a native of Utah now living in Perth, Australia. "She'd get a bit upset that I didn't take it seriously. I told my family once, near the beginning of the pregnancy, 'Oh, Leah's doing quite well. She's not throwing up, at least.' Boy, I got in trouble for that. Soon after, she scripted my response to her physical condition and made me rehearse it: 'Poor Leah. She's sick.' I really meant it the few times I said it thereafter, and it gave me the enormous benefit of knowing exactly what to say for once."

Every so often, a woman exists who is relatively unaffected by the hormonal thrashings of pregnancy. Should your wife stubbornly remain balanced and rational, thereby depriving you of a fatherly rite of passage, try to accept your fate with grace and dignity. After psyching yourself up for spontaneous tears and flying china, if the worst thing your spouse does over the course of the nine months is complain about bunions, you might start seeing mood swings where they don't exist:

SHE: Have you seen my bag? I don't remember where I put it down.
YOU: *Whoa!* Calm down, honey. Take it easy. There's no need to panic.
SHE: I'm not panicking. I'm just trying to find my bag.
YOU: Okay, honey, get ahold of yourself. Just sit down for a minute and take a few deep breaths. This is the hormones talking.

THE DOCTOR FROM ANOTHER ERA: Is Your OB OK?

"The doctor was giving my wife a breast exam on the first visit I ever went to. As he was doing it, it struck me as funny that I was watching this guy fondle my wife's breast. Not in a jealous sort of way, it just struck me as funny. Anyway, as he was doing it, he was asking me a question of some sort. My answer to him was, 'Sorry, Doc, I'm too busy watching you feel up my wife. Should I be looking at you, or what you're doing?'"

—Chad N., Austin, TX

When choosing an obstetrician, an expectant couple must take into account the doctor's experience, references, bedside manner, and hospital affiliation. Obviously. But as the father-to-be, you must not over-look one other important factor: How does the doctor feel about *you*?

Just to be clear, the main purpose of early OB visits is to run di-agnostic checkups—measuring blood pressure, weight gain, and so on—to make sure everything is on track. Honestly, there's really not much for you to do. No one's going to suggest you step in to pump the sphygmomanometer.

For the most part, if you accompany your wife on these trips to the doctor's office, you're in it for the sweeps-week moments, like hearing the fetal heartbeat and seeing the sonogram. Of course, you're also there to comfort your spouse and, perhaps most of all, to gather information. When questions pop up that can't be answered by the stack of books currently bowing the wood of your coffee table, and you don't want to rely solely on the wisdom of katiesmom038@hotmail.com for solutions, these doctor visits provide the chance to probe the mind of a professional. An OB who either ignores or pa-tronizes you is not only useless, but can frustrate you to the point where you start bogarting the stress-relief balls that are intended to be used by the office's pregnant patients.

Things You Don't Want Your Obstetrician to View You as:

The Chauffeur

A nurse opens the door to the waiting room: "Ms. Smith? The doctor will see you now." You and your wife begin to walk to the examining room, when the nurse stops you, shutting the door in your face with, "She'll be out in about twenty minutes."

The Man-Child

While giving your spouse a talk about the rudiments of infant care, the doctor turns to you with a nugget like: "You know, it's going to be very different for you when you have a baby back at the house. I know how hard it can be to pull yourself away from the game, but this little lady here's gonna need some help from time to time."

The Suspect

At various moments throughout the appointment, the doctor glares at you over his clipboard and finally whispers to your wife: "Do you want some privacy? If you're not comfortable with him being here, just say the word."

When some member of the medical community gives you the Neanderthal Dad treatment, you should assert yourself, stand right up, and tell the doctor you're a part of this pregnancy, too. Some obstetricians can be intimidating though, especially the ones who like to slide their bifocals down to the tips of their nose and glare down at you over them like your old first-grade teacher. So making a stand is not always as easy as it might seem. That's when you may want to call upon your wife (who, we hope, is receptive to your feelings—after all, your concern for her is why you're there). A word from the mother-to-be (i.e., "I'd feel so much more comfortable if my husband had all the information, too") might go over much more smoothly when dealing with Dr. Anachronism.

An attempt can be made to avoid such uncomfortable situations altogether by seeking out a doctor with a more progressive view of fatherhood. They're not too hard to find anymore, and a practice's pro-dad stance should be readily apparent from the first visit (lots of hyphenated names in the staff directory, flyers for coed breast-feeding seminars in the waiting room). You can usually increase your odds of finding a father-friendly atmosphere by opting to use a midwife. The college-radio DJs of childbirthing ("Screw you, mainstream poser!"), midwives may very well *expect* you to show up for appointments, and might even hand you some homework on the way out. (Note: Choosing midwifery is not a 100 percent foolproof way to avoid daddy discrimination. One Midwestern father told me of getting the ventriloquist-dummy treatment at an "alternative" birthing center: "Every time I had a question, the midwife would give the answer directly to my wife, as if she was the one who'd asked it.")

If you manage to hook up with a practice that has a "Hooray for fathers!" attitude, there's still something you need to watch out for: You may get *such* a positive reception that you gradually become prone to overly zealous Sensitive Guy behavior just to impress the midwives ("Can you recommend a really good maternity pillow? She says she's comfortable at night, but I'm afraid she's not getting enough between-the-knees support"). I remember making a complete ass out of myself one time when our midwife asked me to step into the waiting room while she conducted a more thorough below-the-belt checkup on my wife. To make sure that the receptionist—and anyone else within earshot—didn't jump to the conclusion that I'd left the examination room out of disinterest, I made sure to inform her that I was off to pee. "And if they finish my wife's pelvic exam before I'm done, please tell them I'll be right back in," I announced. "I don't want to miss anything!"

Aside from causing embarrassment, this kind of overcompensation can also lead to unnecessary anxiety should you, say, feign knowledge of a particular pregnancy-related factoid just to meet what you imagine to be the midwife's growing expectations of you. Before you know it, you're rushing home from an appointment to frantically flip through the *Physicians' Desk Reference* and find out exactly what the hell you signed on for when you confidently blurted out, "Oh, no problem, I'll keep an eye out for any signs of Braxton Hicks." (FYI: Braxton Hicks contractions are short, sporadic tightenings of the uterine muscles, often noticed sometime after midpregnancy, that can make a woman think she's going into early labor. Real contractions are generally much longer, more painful, and occur at regular intervals. See, I've got you covered.)

ABSTINENCE EDUCATION: Everything's Off-limits for Her—What About *You*?

The list of dietary and activity restrictions for pregnant women seems to get longer every year. For moms-to-be, frustration can set in when they are forced—or at least, encouraged—to give up nearly all their tastiest vices. And I'm not just talking about hard-drinkin', chaw-spittin' saloon women. Your wife, too, will find that she has suddenly been cut off from mocha lattes (too much caffeine), tuna steaks (too much mercury), Ring Dings (too many calories), and Gorgonzola (too little pasteurization), just to name a few of the new taboos. And we can't forget the mega-no-no attached to any and all smokable substances. After the mother of your child reads *What to Expect When You're Expecting* (which, unfortunately, they all seem to do), she'll discover that what she should expect is, apparently, a life bereft of personal pleasure.

This new "everything is off-limits" diet presents yet another challenge to the man in her life. If you're out to brunch and you're really craving some eggs Benedict, do you order flapjacks instead, so as not to taunt your wife with the hollandaise sauce that's on her culinary blacklist? If so, your offer of solidarity is quite admirable, but where does it stop? If you join her in abstaining from the hollandaise, because the raw eggs pose a salmonella threat, will you be expected to skip your next pastrami sandwich, too, because deli meats are potential breeding grounds for *Listeria*?

It's best to take your hints from your partner. It's quite possible she won't want you to beg off the goodies from which she's been barred. She may even hope to eat and drink vicariously through you, urging you to consume more and more of her forbidden fruits ("Have another White Russian. Please! I don't care if your vision's gone blurry, I just want to smell the Kahlúa on your breath!"). Go ahead and have fun with this—to a point.

However, should your wife writhe in torment while watching you down espressos, my blunt advice would be: Stop drinking them. When she's around, that is. ("I tried going off caffeine, and my life just fell apart," one West Coast dad lamented.) Whenever you're by yourself, go ahead and make it a banner year for Starbucks. Your wife will likely be touched by your willingness to abstain even part-time. Just don't push it too far by coming home every night stinking of Brie.

That said, we've been talking thus far about abstaining from certain guilty pleasures strictly out of the goodness of your heart. Should you partake of some steak tartare, there's no need to worry about your wife getting secondhand toxoplasmosis. Cigarettes are a different story. When it comes to a dad's personal vices, smoking—of the legal or extra-legal variety—can pose an actual risk to his wife. Unfortunately for the residents of Flavor Country, it is also the hardest to quit (not many people need a shellfish patch to keep them away from raw bars). But doing so is not unprecedented.

Doug M., a dad in Cleveland, was standing outside the hospital with a cigarette in his mouth when, at that moment, he decided to toss the butt and the pack away for good. He bought nicotine gum the next day. "It was just awful; it tasted like I was chewing on some stranger's cigar stub out of an ashtray," he reports. "But I did it for the kid." He hasn't lit up since.

As for that other kind of smoking: Studies have linked marijuana use during pregnancy with children who have memory lapses, attention deficit disorder, and impaired decision-making skills. And secondhand pot smoke does have a potency of its own—if it didn't, shotgunning wouldn't exist. So the (potential) moral of the story here is: Pregnant women + contact high = kid who permanently acts like you do when you're stoned. You can decide for yourself whether you want to take the risk or not. Unless you're high right now, in which case: Have some chips, wait an hour or so, reread this chapter, and then decide.

HELL IS OTHER PEOPLE: The Unfortunate Necessity of Coming Out as an Expectant Dad

The end of the first trimester is often the point in the pregnancy when most couples start spreading the news. You may, of course, opt to come out earlier, as many do—after all, it's certainly tempting to brag about your impending fatherhood. And we should be grateful that our culture has evolved to a point at which men can freely show enthusiasm over the prospect of having a child—and not just in the swaggering, thumbs-through-your-belt-loops, "That's right, boys, I'm all man!" kind of way. But before you blow the whistle on the secret goings-on within your wife's uterus, you should make sure you're aware of what you're getting into.

Many men approach the prospect of parenthood with the adorably naive assumption that it will involve only their children, their spouses, and themselves. In reality, however, as soon as Other People find out you are going to be a parent, they will forcibly insert themselves into your life. The words "We're having a baby" can have a mind-altering effect on people, causing them to infer from that simple declarative sentence that you have just enlisted them as your official child-rearing counsel. You may be taken aback to see how many people, from siblings to baristas to random dudes at the bus stop, seem to look upon the parenting of your future child as a communal experience that gives them a right to voice their opinions. For a guy still trying to sort out his own feelings about the major life change he's undergoing, these kinds of intrusions can drive a father-to-be to distraction.

> "Anybody who's ever held a baby feels like they have the right to tell a father what to do with his kid. The most offensive comment actually came from a nurse in the hospital after my second son was born. When I asked her if I could take the baby to swaddle him, she responded with, 'Either you could do it, or *I* could do it correctly.' You want to talk about infuriating? I'm very proud of my swaddling, but honestly, if you've ever rolled mu shu, you should be able to swaddle a baby."
>
> —Ted H., New York, NY

Not all the people you meet will make you want to pack your bags and go Grizzly Adams. But the folks that can turn your fatherhood into a living purgatory will be out there, too, and announcing to them that you're having a baby is like swimming off the Florida coast wearing a wet suit made of chum. Survival—at least mental survival—depends upon being able to recognize the various types, the way a bushman knows which snakes he can make a hoagie out of and which ones will spit poison into his eye from a hundred paces away.

The Rogues Gallery

Platitude Spewers

These perpetual smilers will be unable to speak more than two sentences without reminding you how blessed you are. Gift-shop wall-plaque slogans will burst forth from them uncontrollably, like some form of PAX TV–sponsored Tourette syndrome.

Typical comment: "We might as well turn off the lights in here, 'cause that little angel inside your wife is making her glow so bright she's just about going to blind us all."

Can be recognized by their: Heads tilted to the side.

May come in the form of: Elderly relatives, supermarket cashiers.

Threat level: Low to high, dependent upon length of encounter.

Unsolicited Mentors

This relentless lot consists of parents—generally of grown children—who will ply you with inappropriate advice that is spoken as if it came verbatim from a pediatrics textbook. Half of what they're saying sounds as if it could possibly be true, the other half like something out of a handwritten manifesto confiscated by FBI agents in a deep-woods shack somewhere. These people may also force you to accept their hand-me-down Nixon-era sharp metal toys and fire-hazard nursery lamps.

Typical comment: "Sometimes when an infant can't sleep it's because their ears are clogged. It's easy to take care of, though. You use turpentine—just a little bit—on the end of a napkin."

Can be recognized by their: Inability to read your expression.

May come in the form of: Family friends, wacky neighbors.

Threat level: Possibly fatal.

Head-Shakers

Always childless themselves, Head-Shakers will riddle you with derisive comments that are supposedly in jest, but seem to carry the actual intent of making you run straight to the nearest adoption agency to sign up your unborn child. Such remarks may be accompanied by a faux punch on the arm. These people sense your impending departure from their lives.

Typical comment: "So I guess it's good-bye to sex for you, huh?"

Can be recognized by their: Rolling eyes, hangovers.

May come in the form of: Barflies, club-hoppers.

Threat level: Low (unless they're lit).

Instant Strangers

Both frustrating and bewildering, these acquaintances of yours will react to the news of your impending parenthood as if you've just told them you'd been receiving top-secret mental memos from telepaths on the asteroid Ceres. Suddenly, they will have no idea what to say to you. At all. Ever again.

Typical comment: ". . ."

Can be recognized by their: Blank stares, slow backward steps.

May come in the form of: Social invalids you used to take pity on.

Threat level: Minimal. Worse for them.

Belly-Touchers

No one knows exactly what drives these people who have a preternaturally poor concept of personal space, but they somehow believe they have been sanctioned to feel your wife. They can strike at any moment, sometimes en masse, making a routine trip to the deli suddenly feel like a scene from *Aliens.* It will be nearly impossible, especially during the last trimester, to walk the aisles of a supermarket or wait in line at an ATM without the

MAKE A LIST, CHECK IT TWICE

When it comes to close friends and family, you really should come clean about the pregnancy before visible clues allow them to figure it out themselves. For an easily offended few, getting the news from anyone other than you could precipitate the kind of relationship rupture that you won't have time to repair once the baby comes. Even the order in which you tell people requires more careful consideration than logic would dictate ("You told Jeff before me? But you and I waited in line for *Lord of the Rings* together! I thought that meant something!"). You might want to take the time to plot out a very specific list. And after everyone has been told, destroy that list.

My mother would have been crushed if she wasn't the first person to know, so I called her first. But she wasn't home. So I immediately called my best friend and told him. Then I called several other people. By the time my mom finally phoned back that evening, I'd already told so many people that I probably announced the pregnancy to her with the same level of excitement that I would the purchase of a new hat. She still assumed she was the first, though, so I let her go right on thinking that. And it's something she will continue to believe. Unless, of course, she reads this.

vigilance of a Secret Service agent, always ready to dive in front of your wife and take a pat on the tummy for her.

Typical comment: *"Oooooh. Awwwww. Ohhhhhh."*

Can be recognized by: Their outstretched arms and shambling zombie-like gait.

May come in the form of: Anyone, anywhere.

Threat level: Medium to high, dependent on their numbers.

Armageddonists

Beware the parents of horrible children, for they would have you believe there is no other kind. Whether it be through lackluster parenting skills or an unfortunate jumble of DNA, these people are stuck with the kind of kids they made horror movies about in the seventies. To make themselves feel better about their hideous offspring, the Armageddonists will speak as if their hell-spawn represent all the children of the world.

Typical comment: "For the first six months, they let you sleep twenty-five or thirty minutes a night. Enjoy it—it only gets worse from there."

Can be recognized by their: Sticky, screaming toddlers punching you repeatedly in the thigh.

May come in the form of: The dried-out husks of once-vibrant people whose company you actually used to find pleasant.

Threat level: To be avoided at all costs.

CHAPTER 2

The Second Trimester

THE APPELLATION TRAIL: Naming Names

My wife and I are geeks. One night, long before conception, we decided to take a break from quizzing each other on trivia from the *World Almanac* ("Okay, name the three most populous countries in South America") to instead pore through a baby name book. (Yes, we had one—I *did* say we were geeks.) We decided upon "Bryn" for a girl and "Caleb" for a boy, choosing those particular names because we liked the sound of them and because they seemed—while not freakish—uncommon enough to prevent our future son or daughter from getting lost in a tempest of Michaels and Emilys. Luckily for Bryn, she turned out to be female, because, quite to our shock, "Caleb" appeared among the top thirty-five boys' names for 2002. If chromosomes had aligned differently, a lack of research on our part might have caused our child to go through elementary school, not simply as Caleb, but as Caleb H.

Most parents spend a bit more time thinking about their child's name than we did. However, naming is one of those pivotal parental decisions in which the world at large seems to believe it has a say. No matter how long and hard you think about your choice, no matter how satisfied you are with it and think it perfectly represents the person you hope your child will be, someone will hate your baby's name.

To demonstrate this point, let us turn—as we do for all things—to the world of entertainment. Back in 2004, when Gwyneth Paltrow named her daughter Apple, the press went ballistic, and coverage surrounding the baby's unconventional name temporarily eclipsed the fact that America was at war. Is Gwyneth Paltrow a terrible mother? Only Apple can say. But she's certainly not a terrible mother *because* she named her baby Apple. Apples are symbolic of good health, they fill America's national pie, and they are the unwavering choice of all children's alphabet books to represent the letter "A." The point is, the impulse-buy magazines of the world felt they had a right to tear Gwyneth Paltrow apart for giving her daughter a name that is really not so bad. Frankly, I've heard much worse (Jason Lee and son Pilot Inspektor, Shannyn Sossamon and daughter Audio Science, Jermaine Jackson and son Jermajesty . . . I'll stop now).

On a side note, where was Chris Martin in all this? Apple's father, as front man of Coldplay, is a celebrity in his own right (though, admittedly, not of the same last-name-optional variety as Gwyneth). That he was not widely mocked in the naming of his own child can be seen as evidence that the media still refuses to accept a man's equal involvement in parenting. I can't speak for Chris Martin (I don't have the accent), but if anyone is incensed enough by my daughter's name to write articles about it, I don't want my wife's name to be the only one in boldface type.

While most of us are not famous enough to have our child's name lambasted in the public sphere, the same thing can happen to every parent on a smaller scale. From friends whose faces squinch up when they first hear the name to relatives who will openly tell you to rethink your choice, negative reactions to baby names are all too common.

Your parents may unsubtly remind you how nice it would be to honor your great-grandfather with a namesake. A confirmed bachelor friend of yours may suggest the obscure Old English name he's always really liked, but knows he, himself, will never have reason to use. A couple you know may have a name they specifically *don't* want you to use, because they hope to claim it for their own child someday (see "The Seven" episode of *Seinfeld*). You will hear of books that speculate about how the first letter of your child's name will determine whether she becomes a peace-brokering diplomat or swimsuit filler in a biker magazine. Religious beliefs or cultural traditions may limit your choice of names. And if any of these factors matter to you, then, by all means, weigh them in your decision.

Remember, though, that you and your wife are the ones who will both hear and say this name more than anyone else—and for that reason alone, you'd better like it. Both of you.

Let's say you really love "Lucius" for a boy and she's against it from the first mention because she dated a guy by that name for three weeks right after college. Her argument may seem trivial, but giving up and moving along might be the preferred course of action. Imagine the day you and your new family bump into old Lucius, only to have him learn your son's name and start slyly nodding in a "That's right, baby, the ladies just can't get over Lucius" kind of way.

There are more names out there than you can shake a copy of *Beyond Jennifer & Jason* at; you will hit upon one you both like. If that doesn't happen, there's always the somewhat risky proposition of going halfsies—you get the boy's name, she gets the girl's. Or vice versa. Or table the discussion until the ultrasound when you can find out the sex of the baby and reduce your name options by 50 percent.

If you make any kind of deals, remember that you have to hold to them. Such was the case for Steve R. of Washington, D.C. "I told my wife that we could name our daughter after Diana, the Roman goddess of the moon—*if* she were born on a full moon," he said. "The baby came suddenly, and in the hours afterward we were frantically looking for newspapers to see what phase the moon was in."

However you decide upon a name, though, just make sure that all possible choices have taken three important factors into account: nicknames ("Hippolyta" may be regal in origin, but shortening it will do your daughter no favors), initials ("Jeremy Alan Zucker" gives your son cool initials, "Jeremy Ian Zucker" does not), and spelling difficulty (despite the fact that "Bryn" has proven to be the absolute perfect name for our daughter, we are now aware of just how often she'll have to correct people's spelling—the most common errors being "Brynn," "Brin," "Brynne," or "Bryan").

You might also want to give serious thought to keeping your choice a secret until after the baby is born. Once there is a little human being attached, people are a lot more likely to accept the name—or even compliment it once they see how well it suits your infant ("Oh, little Velveeta just melts my heart"). And even if people really loathe your selection, they're a lot less likely to voice their displeasure once they know that the emotionally scarring moniker you've saddled your offspring with is already etched onto a birth certificate. At worst, they may say, "That's an interesting name," which is not-so-subtle code for "You have doomed this child to a lifetime of ridicule."

Like everything else, keeping the name secret can have a downside, too, if, say, your chosen name happens to be stolen by someone else's kid before you lay claim to it. "I love Ezra Pound; my wife loves Ezra Jack Keats—so we decided Ezra would be the perfect name for our son, but we didn't tell anyone beforehand," said Dave L. of Columbus, Ohio. "Then, a month before my wife was due, we got a call from our friends across the street who were also expecting. Their baby had just been born and they named him Ezra. We were like, 'No, that's our name!' So for the next few weeks we had to struggle over what to do. But there was no other name we both liked as much. We finally just decided to say, 'The hell with it—there'll be two Ezras.'"

One more important thing to keep in mind is that there's no law requiring you to have a name in place by the time the baby is born. I've spoken to a number of people who waited to see exactly who their child was before deciding on an appropriate name for him. I even know one couple who changed their mind months into their daughter's life; their little girl is now three and is a happy, smart, emotionally well-adjusted child. To be honest, there are probably countless infants out there who, in the first year of life, assume their names are Sweetie, Honey, or Kiddo, anyway. And besides, your child could always end up hating her own name and having it legally changed as soon as she turns eighteen, which is a risk we all must take.

LET'S GET PHILOSOPHICAL: What Makes a Good Parent?

Choosing your child's name is one of the first mega-decisions you make as a parent, but it is only the beginning. If you haven't already done so by this point, you will soon begin to ask yourself, "So, how exactly do I raise a child?"

Will spankings make her respect authority, or cause her to rebel later in life? Will allowing the baby to sleep in your bed strengthen his bonds with you, or make him indescribably needy? Does allowing an infant to cry teach her to calm herself or to hate you? Is any

THE THING WITHOUT A NAME

My wife and I ran into an unforeseen dilemma around the topic of naming: What do we call the baby while in utero? Since we opted not to learn the sex of the child until the birth, we didn't want to use either the male or female name we'd chosen, nor did we feel comfortable constantly referring to our future child as "it" (no associations with Stephen King monsters, please). Somehow, we arrived at "Spoon" as the perfect temporary name for our unborn child—and considering the head-to-body-size ratio at that stage of development, it wasn't entirely inappropriate. (Incidentally, the day after the birth, in the hospital room, I used the word "spoon" without thinking about it, as in: "Please pass me that spoon so I can eat my cafeteria Jell-o." I swear to you, Bryn's eyes lit up.)

It seems pretty common for fetal nicknames to sound utterly random, but occasionally there's an origin story behind them. California dad Alex P. and his wife chose one based on their child's sonogram performance: "The baby could barely be seen, she was zipping around so much: You'd catch a glimpse of a leg, then a hand for a second, then some ribs, then she was off again. She carried the nickname 'Turbobaby' until she was born."

Don't get too attached to a prebirth label, though. No one ever called our daughter Spoon after she was born, even though, all along, I had been expecting that her in-the-womb nickname would stick throughout her childhood and perhaps far beyond ("Where's my little grandspoon?"). Spoon had been a purely hypothetical child, but now Bryn was here, a real baby with a personality all her own. Spoon couldn't compete.

TV acceptable besides *Veggie Tales*? The answers to these kinds of inflammatory questions are what makes up, as it's called these days, one's Parenting Philosophy.

For answers, the modern parent turns to the gurus. With a quick Google search for the term "parenting," you will see that hundreds of experts, with varying levels of qualification, are out there offering up their own personal recipes for raising the perfect child. And there are countless different parenting philosophies for you to explore. Here, we will discuss the only two that people ever talk about.

A Gross Oversimplification of the Two Dominant Parenting Philosophies

Attachment Parenting: Popularized by the prolific Dr. William Sears (author of *The Baby Book,* that gigantic big blue tome you've seen next to the slightly thinner pink one, *The Pregnancy Book*), attachment parenting, appropriately enough, means being attached to your child at all times. You wear the baby, sleep with the baby, never leave the baby's sight, generally give the baby whatever she wants whenever she wants it, and never *ever* let the baby cry. Veering even slightly from this formula will result in your infant growing up to be an emotionally stunted sociopath.

The Ferber Method: With a theory centered almost solely around sleep issues, Dr. Richard Ferber *(Solve Your Child's Sleep Problems)* is the archnemesis of attachment parents, due to his assertion that a baby should be trained to sleep well—a process which entails letting her bawl her way through the night until she is overcome by exhaustion. Failing to implement the "Cry It Out" technique, as it has been dubbed, will leave you with a child, who at the age of forty, not only still lives with you but crawls, shivering, under the covers with you anytime the big angry dog next door barks at a squirrel.

In reality, attachment parenting doesn't actually call for your child to keep breast-feeding until prom night, nor does Ferberization actually state that parents should turn up the volume on their surround sound to drown out the banshee-like wails emanating from the nursery. And neither of the above doctors claims that following the other's theory will result in serial killers or shut-ins. No, it is the more insane adherents of these philosophies who resort to flaming one another on Internet message boards, labeling one another as enablers or neglecters, and using epithets that would result in hefty fines should the FCC start regulating the Web.

Only these most fanatical few look upon one particular theory as gospel and follow its advice to the letter. Most couples end up crafting their own DIY philosophy. They pluck a little bit from Column A, a little bit from Column B, and a little bit from all the other authors, as well as all the parenting magazines, the Web sites, and even the random people who sit next to them on airplanes. And you can generally expect to get *something* you like from any of these sources (I was particularly grateful to Dr. Sears for imparting the commonsense fact that infants don't need real shoes until they can walk). Though you should also expect to come across a few jaw-droppers (like another suggestion from Sears that working parents set up a playpen at the office so they can bond with their little one on the job).

But, you might ask, if all these experts can't seem to reach a consensus about how children should be cared for, how can my wife and I ever expect to? The answer is that it pays for the experts to disagree. No one gets a book published by saying, "Dr. Spock nailed it in '46. 'Nuff said." They need to stake their fame on something new, revolutionary, perhaps even zany. When it comes to parenting manuals, the perpetuation of the species is based on authors saying, "Hey, there are all these books out there that tell you how to raise your kid, yet you still don't know what to do, so why not try mine now?" Without experts contradicting one another, the parenting-advice industry would be dead.

Unlike you and your wife, the gurus don't have a vested interest in teamwork. Sears isn't relying on Ferber to point out an overlooked wad of poop dangling from his elbow after a hasty diaper change (as far as we know, at least). But in your own relationship, where a lack of compromise can mean the difference between a peaceful home and a pit-fighting arena, a desire to find common ground pays off.

Plus, after your baby arrives, and you discover that your unique child doesn't fit neatly into any one template set forth by any one book, you and your spouse will end up winging it most of the time anyway. "I read so many books before my son was born," said Alex E. from Brooklyn, "and I got so tired of the fact that all the information was contradictory. I might as well have asked a hundred random people I passed on the street how I should raise my child. Reaching that breaking point was good, though, because learning to reject professional advice has made me much more comfortable with myself as a parent."

IN THE BEDROOM: What About Sex?

Okay, let's assume you're not one of those men whose delusions of grandeur and lack of a working knowledge of female anatomy cause you to worry about giving the fetus a poke in the eye during intercourse. Still, sex during pregnancy can be a bit of an enigma—enticing and intimidating at the same time. Even if you're the type of guy who can get turned on by a Lands' End catalog, you still might be a little trepidacious about pregnant sex. And with good reason. A lot has changed since the last time you and your wife were under the sheets (or on the bathroom floor, or on a pool table, or wherever you were).

Let's start with the obvious fact that a woman who has gained thirty to forty pounds might develop some body-image issues. She may also be exhausted, nauseous, and more flatulent than the cowboys at the cookout in *Blazing Saddles.* Her back, legs, and head may ache, too. Oh, and she might have sore breasts. In short, she's not always going to be in the mood.

Bracing yourself for that likelihood from the start will help you better appreciate those moments when your partner comes gunning to get you in the sack. A pregnant woman's sex drive can flit in and out like the reception on an old rabbit-eared television set, but when it comes in, it can kick into hyperdrive. The second trimester is your best bet for three months of solid Cinemax action. So for those of you who fear you'll be forced to live like a cloistered monk for the better part of a year, there's no need to get so dire.

And if you're one of the many guys who anticipate that their sexual desire for their wives will wane, but still plan to do the right thing and be ever at the ready with a "Honey, you look fantastic," you may be pleasantly surprised by how little you have to fake it. Something raw and primal kicks in when a woman's body starts rounding out over the course of a pregnancy; perhaps it's the product of some sort of pheromone released along with that famous "maternal glow," perhaps it's that her cup size jumps a few letters down the alphabet. There's a reason why those Renaissance artists fixated on nudes with curvy hips and voluptuous breasts: It's a classic standard for female beauty. And pregnant women have got it in spades.

"My wife feels big and bloated; between fertility drugs and the baby weight, she's gained quite a bit," one dad-to-be told me. "I can't keep my hands off her."

Perhaps surprisingly, I heard from many men for whom the issue was not difficulty in getting aroused by their partner's larger figure, but a certain discomfort with exactly *how* excited they got by it. They couldn't quite put their finger on why their suddenly super-sized wives were setting their loins a-tingle. Some feared that they were developing a fetish; that perhaps long after the pregnancy was over they might find themselves spending their nights hunched over a computer, scrolling through the thumbnail galleries at Naked Preggos.com. They got over their concerns, though. And should you find yourself in the same rockin' boat, you probably will, too. After all, this is your wife: Getting turned on by her is generally not a bad thing.

"My wife reported to me that sex during pregnancy gave her much more powerful orgasms," one Southern dad confessed. "I was happy to indulge her."

Should the opposite be true, and you find that your partner's pregnant body is, for one reason or another, less attractive to you, you are not a freak. Other guys go through the same thing. And based on what they were willing to tell me—or write about on Internet message boards, which often serve as clearinghouses for paternal sex woes—they feel terrible about the fact that they're the ones putting a halt on the bedroom activity in their household. A lot of guys anticipate the possibility that their wife will lose interest in intercourse, but they don't expect to be the ones saying, "Not tonight." The fact is, baby thoughts can get in the way of X-rated thoughts.

"When my wife was first pregnant, we had pretty good sex," said Shannon F. of Chesapeake, Virginia. "We figured there was no risk of getting pregnant, so we went for it. Then, it stopped cold the first time I felt the baby move. I was overjoyed to feel the little bugger kick—but in *that* moment, 'it' was no longer a concept but a person. I loved my wife, but I found it hard to get 'it' out of my mind when considering sex."

Having a child enter your life is a major change, so give yourself some leeway if images of infants keep popping into your head at inopportune times. It might help to make sure no illustrated lactation-consultant brochures are sitting out in plain view while you're trying to get down to business.

If you're not feeling driven to tear your partner's clothes off, another possible reason could be that those clothes are all muumuus and baggy sweatsuits. Many women, eager to adopt the trappings of pregnancy, dive right into maternity wear the moment their bellies are big enough to hold up the elastic waistband of a pair of oversize stirrup pants. You might want to try shopping for her or with her. I never did so myself, but I wish I had thought of it during my wife's pregnancy, if only to provide myself with an alternative to the regular appearance of her Laura Ingalls–style nightgown. There are genuine designers making maternity clothes today, so there's really no reason why a pregnant woman has to automatically start dressing like a colonial grandmother or an extra from *Sweatin' to the Oldies*.

However you feel about your wife's body during the pregnancy, chances are your desire to get laid hasn't gone anywhere. Difficulty getting aroused by the woman you want to sleep with is certainly an obstacle, but one that can be overcome. One guy I spoke to was very blunt about how his wife's pregnancy affected his sexual desire for her, as well as how he got past the problem: "Frankly, I'm not into big bodies. For a while she just didn't do anything for me. But we still had sex. I just had to use my imagination."

And that's the key, several dads told me. Focus on the parts of your partner that still turn you on: eyes, neck, wrists, back. Get the blood flowing beforehand with outside visual aids (available in paper, video, and electronic formats). And like our anonymous friend said above, use your imagination. If *Penthouse*'s "I never thought it would happen to me . . ." letters have taught us anything, it is that sexual fantasy is not a problem for most men. If you can call upon that creativity when you're alone, you should be able to use it when you're with your wife.

If you're horny and she's horny, go for it. For those nine months of pregnancy, you need to keep your eyes open for any possible coital opportunities, and don't let any slip you by. Once you're living with a baby, logistics will trump lust, and the plain truth is that you just won't have as much time for extracurricular activities.

Also, take advantage of the opportunity presented by the belly. It poses difficulties only if you remain a stubborn missionary man. Do not think of the protruding abdomen as an obstacle; consider it instead a sort of silent but persistent *Kama Sutra* instructor, forcing you to explore new, more challenging positions, the likes of which you may never have previously considered, but which you may find yourself, in the afterglow, mentally jotting down for inclusion in your permanent repertoire.

THE ULTRASOUND AND THE FURY:
The Rigors of Prenatal Testing

Years after the birth of a child, most people can look back upon the more difficult points of a pregnancy and laugh—even about parts that were decidedly unfunny when they first occurred ("Hey, remember when you vomited so hard your capillaries burst, and I said they looked like freckles, and you kicked me in the groin? Ah, those were crazy times"). The prenatal testing period is usually not among those fond memories.

The light-speed progress of medical science seems to result in the invention of a new prenatal test every three weeks or so. And while information is good, too much information is not always so. Some tests are required by law in certain states, other diagnostics come highly recommended (i.e., might as well be law, according to your doctor), and then there are those in the ever-increasing stockpile of elective tests. I'm not going to go into detail on all the various forms of pregnancy testing available, because there are bound to be at least forty-seven new tests created between the writing and publishing of this book.

But medical testing is serious business. Remembering that fact is the main challenge for parents-to-be, especially when it comes to the crème-de-la-tests, the ultrasound, or sonogram. Prescribed somewhere in the twelve-to-twenty-week range for the average pregnancy, this is the test that allows you a first glimpse of your future child. Because of the fact that you can walk away with a snapshot of your fetus—even if it more closely resembles a sonar charting of the Great Barrier Reef than a photograph of a baby—many couples approach the sonogram with the jauntiness of a visit to the Sears Portrait Studio, rather than the gravity of a medical screening for birth defects.

Without doubt, the most stressful days of my wife's pregnancy were the few following our twentieth-week ultrasound. It started out all excitement and anticipation: At the hospital the technician lubed up my wife's belly with purple goop and then, as she ran her mechanical magic wand over the abdomen, we sat glued to the monitor looking for anything with a vaguely humanoid shape. The thrill of finally seeing little hand- and feet-like thingies was undeniable; even more so was the profile of the face (which I thought—and stupidly blurted out—resembled me). Then the mood in the room took a very quick downward turn as the technician brought the test to a halt and dashed off without explanation to fetch a doctor. Already unnerved, we were pretty much dumbstruck when the physician who completed the testing focused the picture on one specific area of the baby's anatomy: "You see that white spot on the heart? That could be a problem."

The next thing we knew, we were ushered in to see a genetic counselor, who explained to us that the echogenic focus (the little smudgy area) on our sonogram was considered a potential marker for Down syndrome. The only way to know for sure, we were told, was to have an amniocentesis performed—that's the test where amniotic fluid is drained from the uterus through a long needle in the woman's abdomen. We were also informed that the amnio itself carried a risk of miscarriage, anywhere from 0.3-to-3 percent (depending on whom you ask). The choice of how to proceed was ours to make.

My wife and I both had the benefit of journalism backgrounds, so as soon as we were able to shake off the initial shock of the news, our natural instinct was to dive into research. Through the rabid study-ing of stats and the reading of numerous articles and medical-journal studies (especially one specific report that our genetic counselor had pointed us toward), we learned that what they call soft markers for Down syndrome, among which the echogenic focus is included, are incredibly common. As many as one in five sonograms shows a marker. Only about one in one thousand babies has Down syndrome.

We realized that multiple markers—or markers paired with other abnormalities, like misshapen fetal body parts—pointed to a much higher possibility for birth defects, but in our case, with only one marker, the chance of our baby having the condition was smaller than the risk of miscarriage through amniocentesis. Putting the test results in context was the key to handling the worries that we'd abruptly been saddled with.

I've run into a large number of other parents who've gone through similar ordeals. The health of your baby is one of the most obvious concerns you can have as an expectant father; and this kind of test-induced anxiety is all too common. It's also unnecessary, since the results are often not definitive—they only suggest further testing. The same is true of many other prenatal tests. Knowledge of that little detail is essential to maintaining one's composure during this period.

The alpha-fetoprotein test, or AFP, is one of those tests that can easily provide you with freak-out-inducing results. It is an incredibly common blood screening used to detect numerous birth defects of varying degrees of severity—one of those tests that some states legally insist upon. However, it's got an outlandishly high false-positive rate. While always a bit disarming to hear that your wife's AFP results point toward a potential defect, remember that it does not mean the sky is falling. Just get more tests—more noninvasive tests, of which there are plenty—to help put your mind at ease. And get as much info about the tests as possible. Ask about complication rates, the likelihood of incorrect results, anything you think you might want to know. Annoy your doctors. What you want to avoid is information without context.

Also, if it turns out that an amniocentesis must be done, try to take it in stride. For women over thirty-five, most doctors will recommend one anyway. While there is that slight chance that the test itself could cause problems, the odds are still heavily on your side. Most books and experts seem to agree that it might be more useful to find out your particular hospital's or doctor's error rate, since bad or inexperienced physicians raise the national averages. Amnio is probably the most accurate test available, so should your wife have to undergo the procedure, it will likely put all doubts to rest.

And there you have it: the Cliffs Notes version of one of the heavier topics you're likely to come across in pregnancy literature. Now let's move on to discuss what it feels like to speak into a woman's navel.

CAN YOU HEAR ME NOW?: Getting to Know Your Fetus

> "Several times a week I would bend over and say something to the belly, close enough that the baby probably heard some sort of booming voice. I had always assumed that I would slap some headphones on my wife's belly and play good music—Mozart, or maybe Sting—but never got around to it. It was more fun to talk to the belly, anyway."   —Steve R., Washington, D.C.

At the risk of sounding cheesy or overly sentimental, I admit I had regular conversations (albeit one-sided ones) with my wife's belly during her pregnancy. I like to believe the studies that claim a newborn has the ability to recognize voices he first heard in the womb. I'm sure that from inside the uterus, where your voice has to be heard through several layers of fluid, flesh, and muscle, you sound like Charlie Brown's teacher at best. But I find it reasonable that if the baby hears your voice frequently enough, the timbre of it could become familiar to him. There's a big difference, though, between hoping your infant will turn his head toward you when you call his name in the delivery room (which on a fundamental level, amounts to nothing more than a parlor trick), and treating your fetus to pre-natal sonatas in hopes of turning the kid into a Doogie Howser–like prodigy.

When it comes to in utero education, there are two distinct schools of thought—the first being that the intricate composition of classical music will stimulate growth in the spatial-learning centers of your baby's brain, the second being that the first is a load of crap. The Mozart Effect (not to be confused with *Baby Mozart* videos, which work very well at keeping your child occupied while you brush your teeth) is still an unproven theory. Even the parents who take the time to play symphonies for their unborn children seem to do so with a bit of skepticism ("At least it got me to listen to classical," said one). Whether there is any truth to the benefits or not, it definitely won't hurt to expose your unborn baby to a philharmonic every now and then. Just don't be disappointed if you spend six months of your wife's pregnancy with the Brandenburg concertos on repeat and your infant still attempts to force the oval block into the star hole on his Playskool shape sorter.

When it comes to interaction with the yet-to-be-born, at the very least, you know you want to feel the kicks. Everybody wants to feel the kicks. And sometimes it will seem like everybody else gets to feel them before you. It's easy to grow jealous—not only of your wife who talks constantly about how the baby is hoofing it like a little Savion Glover under her maternity dress, but also of anybody else who happens to be around when she announces a kick storm brewing and can effortlessly pinpoint the exact area of movement ("Wow, that was a big one!"). Envy will develop if every time you attempt to do the same, you spend what feels like an eternity running your hands along every inch of abdomen and coming up empty. Your frustration will only be compounded if your wife begins to pity your fruitless attempts to feel the kicks:

SHE: *Ooh!* There she goes again. Quick, come feel!
YOU: Where? Where?
SHE: Right there.

YOU: Where my hand is?

SHE: Yeah, right there.

YOU: Did she stop?

SHE: No. Still going. Don't you feel it?

YOU: What am I supposed to be feeling?! Where is it?!

SHE: It's stopped, honey. She's done. She's resting. It's over. Just go sit down. Please.

Stick with it, though. You will eventually catch a kick.

It helps to think of these snipe hunts as an introduction to the way your child can drive you crazy by not doing what you want. And *that* is a particular breed of frustration with which you will soon become very well acquainted.

CHAPTER 3

The Third Trimester

PRIDE AND PREGNANCY: How Much Help Is Too Much?

"I take care of things at home; I cook, clean, do laundry, mow, plus more. I also take care of my grandparents and my mother-in-law. If anything, I would say that my pregnant wife has wanted me to lay off and allow her to do more."

—Billy S., Dix, IL

As the pregnancy progresses, unless your wife's got a green card from the planet Krypton, she will need a little bit of a hand here and there. While many guys these days do their fair share of household chores, helping out during the pregnancy means more than doubling your time with the Swiffer. By the third trimester, a woman may have physical difficulty pulling on her pants, bending over to pick up a dropped set of keys, or extracting herself from a papasan chair.

You probably have some idea as to where your wife naturally falls on the Female Independence Scale—a fluid spectrum spanning all the way from Blanche DuBois to Xena, Warrior Princess. I'm going to go out on a limb here and say that most women will fall somewhere in the middle and have no problem accepting any assistance their husbands are willing to offer during the pregnancy.

But those of you with a partner who milks her purported invalid status to the point at which you essentially become her manservant may suspect that she might be taking advantage of you. Too many requests for you to open window shades, fill glasses of water, and take on other tasks that could be competently performed by an anemic six-year-old may make you begin to doubt the legitimacy of your wife's pleas. Like the defense lawyer in an insurance fraud case who stakes out an accident victim's home in hopes of catching the guy practicing Tae Bo in his neck brace, you may be on the lookout for proof that your wife is not as incapacitated as she claims to be ("*Aha!* So you *can* reach the remote by yourself!"). Loss of trust can deal a harsh blow to a relationship, so you need to tackle this problem quickly. Just talk about it with her. A few mothers I know (my wife included) have explained to me that even the most confident woman can feel more vulnerable than usual during pregnancy. She may ask for you to do some things that she could do herself, because seeing you do them is reassuring to her, and lets her know you are there for her in her time of need.

Word of warning: Even if you've become the most helpful husband in America, make sure you don't develop a martyr complex about it. While your wife will appreciate your extra effort, anybody else from whom you might be seeking some sympathy is not going to care. Any temptation to recount your daily chores as if they were the seven labors of Hercules can be a quick road to pariah status: "Man, you should see what I've got to do around the house now. I'm in the kitchen for hours—and I'm not usually the one who cooks. I've had to learn everything from scratch. You ever try to fold an omelet? Not easy. But that's only after I clean out the bathtub—

which I don't mind doing, of course. I couldn't let her get on her hands and knees in her condition; it's not even a consideration. . . ." See, you're insufferable.

If the woman you're with resides comfortably at the turbo-charged end of the Feminine Independence Scale, her admirable strength and self-confidence are most likely major components of your attraction to her. But in the unique situation of a pregnancy, when your natural inclination to fall into helper/protector/caregiver mode kicks in, you may find that the very traits that drew you to this woman in the first place have suddenly become obstacles.

Say she drops the issue of *Jane* she's reading. You immediately jump up to retrieve it for her, only to be waved away with, "Relax, I can get it." She then proceeds to work up a sweat in the simple process of bending over, straining to reach past her belly and eliciting the kinds of grunts and groans you've only previously heard during a Williams sisters match. And yet, you still don't know whether to step in or not.

> "Up until the ninth month, my wife would dust. If I tried to step in, she felt controlled and she'd get pissed. I called it the Pregnancy Snap."   —Dave L., Columbus, OH

If you already know your wife is not the type who will react peaceably to hearing that she can't handle the amount of work she's doing, personally, I'd avoid taking the blunt route. Instigating confrontation with a woman in her third trimester is generally ill-advised. Over the course of the pregnancy, some member of the medical community will undoubtedly warn you that stress is harmful to the fetus. They will tell you that the mother-to-be should endeavor to avoid any exposure to anxiety-inducing situations—a piece of advice that is, on the whole, pointless, since telling a pregnant woman not to get stressed is about as useful as telling a Bengal tiger to lay off red meat. Nonetheless, since your goal is to reduce strain and tension for your wife, it's generally better not to initiate the kind of "discussion" that you suspect would result in an argument (unless, of course, you're like those 1940's newspaper folk who used snappy rapid-fire bickering as a form of foreplay).

Instead, you could just try telling her you *want* to help. During a woman's pregnancy, the man can feel pretty damn useless: *She* carries around the extra weight for nine months, *she* has to cope with morning sickness, *she* has to adjust her daily routine to accommodate hourly bathroom visits. And these are all things she doesn't have much choice about; they're biologically driven. By contrast, anything the man does is entirely voluntary.

This gives you ample justification in begging your wife to let you help her out, to let you do more so that you feel like you are a part of what's going on. Make the need yours, not hers. This kind of earnest vulnerability, while not natural for every man, goes a long way with many women, and can be an easy road to earning that coveted position of Involved Partner while safeguarding her ego in the process. If that doesn't work, pass the buck. After one expectant father's plea met continued resistance, he decided to make a move at their next prenatal visit: "I just asked the obstetrician, 'Please explain to my wife that she can't do everything.'" It worked.

If all else fails, you can always enter covert operative mode. Help her before she can stop you. Or before she even notices. This is a *pregnant* woman we're talking about, so you're likely to find ample time to clean, cook, and shop without attracting any unwanted attention (e.g., while she's taking her fifth nap of the day, while she's engrossed in the latest edition of *Baby Bargains,* or while she's at the office explaining to her coworkers why she doesn't need *their* extra help). This can make the entire experience more exciting, as it finally gives you a chance to test your skills at military-style strategy and ninja-like stealth.

Whatever your path to partnership, whether out in the open or under cover of darkness, you need to take into account your own personal limits. There is a potential danger in performing too well. Just like the kicker who plays phenomenally all season but misses the final field goal of the Super Bowl and sees himself being burned in effigy by shirtless, face-painted fans before he can even leave the stadium, the husband who sets too high a standard for himself during the pregnancy may be seen as a loafing slacker once the baby's in the picture and there's actually far more work for him to do.

"I did a lot of extra housework while my wife was pregnant," one brand-new dad reported. "Since the baby came, though, not so much. I think somebody's not too happy about that."

Please keep in mind that we're not talking about being callous or lazy here. As has been stated above, there's only so much the man can do during the pregnancy, while after the birth, there's a whole lot more (diapering, burping, holding, calming, entertaining, feeding, bathing, snot-wiping, vomit-catching) that we guys can take part in. This puts us in a much more meaningful role as a parent, but it also means that it may be physically impossible for us to still dust the venetian blinds eight times a week. This is simple reality, but in appearance, it may look to some as if we've picked up the baby and dropped everything else. To avoid such misunderstanding, you can either make sure you don't spend the entire gestation period running around like the Flash and creating unrealistic expectations for your future self, or you can sit down and explain the situation to your wife. While the latter is the nobler of the two paths, the success of such a conversation may depend on whether it's high or low tide in the ever-shifting sea of hormones upon which your spouse is currently adrift.

SHOWER POWER: The Joy of Getting

It used to be that baby showers were strictly female territory. For most men, they were as mysterious as Freemason initiation rituals. What went on behind those particular closed doors was a complete unknown, though it was generally assumed to include lots of ribbon and carry a vaguely floral scent. Today, the "No Boys Allowed" signs are beginning to come down. Coed showers are becoming increasingly common.

"I surprised my wife with a baby shower on the morning of Super Bowl Sunday," said Keith R. of Boston. "I knew it would be the one time I could surprise her, because I would never plan *anything* on Super Bowl Sunday."

One dad-to-be from rural Illinois told me that he is not just attending a shower, he's put himself in charge of invitations, decorations, and cakes. Some men recoil at such thoughts, but these naysayers, even if they're not teeming with enthusiasm for the event, are overlooking two big pluses to a coed shower. First of all, for the man who plans to be (and wants to be seen as) an involved father, this is your chance to set precedent. The shower is likely to be the first big event centered around your child; your presence there sends a message. "We felt it was important to have a coed shower," said Bill T. from Brooklyn, "because, right from the beginning, that started us off in the vein that the baby is not just Mommy's responsibility."

Then, of course, there's also the more pragmatic benefit: more genders = more guests = more gifts.

With all the fun baby goods to shop for (Ramones bibs; Che Guevara jumpers), no new father wants to have to spend his own time and money buying socks, washcloths, and wipe warmers. So why not let second cousins, cubicle-mates, and minor acquaintances purchase that boring stuff for you? If you in any way feel guilty about sending these folks out to find you a spare bottle brush, keep in mind that you will at some point have to buy a gift of equal mundanity for most of them, whether it's for their own baby shower, a wedding, housewarming, or dog's christening. You can also calm your conscience by making sure your registry contains a gift for every price range, from leather-padded high chairs down to plastic spoons.

Registering for shower gifts is as pivotal to having babies today as newspapers and hot water were to the process in old movies. Assuming that a good 50 percent of your guests will buy whatever the hell *they* want anyway, a registry—much appreciated by your lazier or less creative friends—is the only way of ensuring you get anything you actually need. Another benefit of registering: If no one comes forward to offer their services as party planner (usually an old friend of your wife's, who jumps up with Kelly Ripa–level enthusiasm and shouts, "I'm going to throw you the best baby shower EVER!"), dropping casual asides to people about which store holds your registry is also a pretty clear way of saying, "*Helloooo.* We're waiting to be feted over here." While this could easily come across as obnoxious in the real world, the arbitrary etiquette of parenthood has for some reason deemed the practice acceptable.

Or you can always just host the party yourself. It's good to hold this option as a backup plan if you and your wife are the first among your circle of friends to have a baby. Nonparents are often quite clueless about this type of thing and even the most blatant hints you throw their way might bounce right off their brains.

COMMENT FROM YOU: We set up a baby registry on Amazon, because we figured that would make it really easy for anyone to do their shower shopping.

HOPED-FOR RESPONSE: Oh, hey, who's throwing you guys a shower? Because if nobody's on top of that yet, I'd love to start getting some plans together.

ACTUAL RESPONSE: *Ooh,* that reminds me, I haven't updated my Wish List in, like, forever. *The Da Vinci Code* is probably still on there.

However you get the event to happen, the only big issue left to tackle is: friends or family? A baby shower with your and your wife's friends as the core guest group can be practically indistinguishable from a pleasant cocktail party, except for the presence of tiny booties. If extended family gets involved in the planning, though, expect a generally frillier aesthetic, more guessing games about your wife's weight, and *Wheel of Fortune*–esque oohing and ahhing.

Since friends and family rarely mix well, the easiest solution is to have two showers. Let your tradition-happy relatives throw you the old-fashioned coo-fest they've been dying for, then invite all your friends and coworkers to the swingin'est baby shower since the birth of Nancy Sinatra. You can even make separate registries, target-marketing specific gift requests to the invitees most likely to buy them. Great-Aunt Myrna will have no problem presenting you with a stack of plain white onesies ("You'll go through those like Kleenex!"), while your friend with the huge vinyl LP collection may get excited about the John Lennon line of crib blankets.

The shower by one's peers, while not without its challenges (barbs are thrown between the two people who both give you a copy of *Pat the Bunny,* you run out of artichoke dip, etc.), is essentially just a party. The family shower is another animal altogether. Even if it's being called "coed" (i.e., "Okay, okay, your husband can come"), you still might be the only guy there. Given the choice, older male relatives will often either stay home or all congregate together around the nine-inch Sony in the kitchen to watch a PGA tournament. They will be given a free pass to do so, but as a guest of honor you will be expected to be present for the main festivities. Therefore, you must prepare to be uncomfortable.

A few suggestions for getting through the family shower without the use of pharmaceuticals:

- Practice your "excited face" at home before you go, so you don't deflate some septuagenarian's good time with your lackluster re-action to a freshly unwrapped nursing bra.
- Pocket your pride for the day: Someone *will* put a bow on your head.
- Expect your presence at the event to be used as justification for older female relatives to insult their own spouses. ("I tell you, I never thought I'd live to see a husband coming to a shower. Your wife's Uncle Ted, he couldn't have cared less. He didn't even realize I'd given birth until two weeks after I brought the baby home.")
- Get your ego prepped for repeated, but unintentional insult: Despite the awe inspired by your mere presence, these older women will still assume you know absolutely nothing. ("Those are wipes, dear. Diaper wipes. For wiping the baby. When you change his diaper. Put them back in the bag so you don't lose them.")

- Remain goal-oriented: Never forget that you are dealing with all this in exchange for having someone other than you purchase a slipcover for your changing table.

A third option is for you and the missus to go your separate ways; she has her fiesta, you have yours. The slightly more effete cousin of the Bachelor Party, the Man Shower has its own unique pitfalls: barbecue-sauce stains, welts on your back from all the half-smacking man-hugs, generally crappier presents. But you can rest assured that no one attending will expect a thank-you card.

If you're worried about receiving a whole bunch of second-rate gifts, you can avoid that problem in one of two ways. The first is to make sure you invite some guys who already have kids; they'll know a good baby present when they see one. The alternative is to follow the route that one Kansas City dad-to-be took and make your Man Shower a Diaper Party. Diapers are one thing you know you'll need a lot of, no matter what, so give your guests a break by telling them exactly what to bring, while adding to your stockpile of Pampers at the same time.

Perhaps the biggest danger with the Man Shower, though, is the potential for overcompensation. You're cramming a lot of testosterone into one room and, unlike their female counterparts, attendees of a guys-only gathering are far more likely to, at some point in the evening, forget why this shindig is being thrown in the first place. Not that the festivities will necessarily devolve into Delta House shenanigans. Still, the majority of these events will involve both a few cases of Pabst Blue Ribbon and at least one friend who views this as his last chance to see you drunk. I'm sure you can do the math.

WHAT YOU NEED: Stuff

> "We are grabbing every parenting product we can get our hands
> on. Sometimes it feels like we're preparing for a hurricane
> rather than a baby."   —Jeff H., Brooklyn, NY

Back in the olden days, when you were about to have a baby, you'd
need maybe a couple of bottles, something to mash peas with, a pile
of swaddling, and you were good to go. Today, they won't even allow you to take the baby home from the hospital unless you can show
proof that you've accumulated at least one metric ton of choking-
hazard-free merchandise. Stuff (and I use that term in the George
Carlin sense) is a major part of modern parenting.

Registering—or worse yet, doing your own shopping—for baby
products can be almost as overwhelming to expectant fathers as the
prospect of the birth itself. The baby-goods industry has never offered a more voluminous array of options, and the whirlwind of bottle warmers, teething rings, and tummy-time mats can be quite
disorienting. You shouldn't let your drive to provide your baby with
the safest, most developmentally enriching products on the market
bankrupt you before you get a chance to open your child's 527
college savings account. Unfortunately, since the flooding of your
home with unnecessary kid stuff is virtually inevitable, here are
some thoughts on a few of the most important new-parent acquisi-
tions.

- **Someplace for the Baby to Sleep:** Cribs, bassinets, cradles, Moses
  baskets—I've known people who've crowded their homes with
  several or even all of these items, assuming they each serve a different purpose. They don't. The latter three all distinguish them-

selves from the crib by providing a smaller sleeping area, which purportedly makes them a more familiar-feeling nest for a newborn who has just spent nine months confined to a very tiny space. Amongst themselves, though, this trio just represents different gradations of the same product. They can be compared to the holy trinity of Mars candy bars: 3 Musketeers contains plain nougat; add caramel and you've got Milky Way; when peanuts enter the picture, it's Snickers. Same with the bedding: A Moses basket is a soft little repository in which a baby can sleep; make it rock and it's a cradle; add legs or a stand of some kind and you have a bassinet.

So it really all comes down to a question of "Big sleeping thing or little sleeping thing?" Since your child will eventually grow out of the more diminutive bedtime unit, a crib will probably be a necessity at some point. Therefore, if your kid can handle it, you can save time, space, and money by bypassing the smaller baby beds completely. But what of the comfort infants are supposed to derive from an enclosed sleeping area? Well, it depends on the child—just like adults, babies often refuse to conform to generalizations. My wife and I got a bassinet *and* a crib, assuming we would use the lesser unit until Bryn was ready to transition to the full-size one; turned out, Bryn really liked to sprawl out in bed and being confined within a tight space was, for her, about as conducive to slumber as the sweet lullaby of a jackhammer. After three ill-fated attempts at using the bassinet for its intended purpose, it was demoted to the role of rocking laundry hamper.

- **Something to Change the Baby On:** Anybody who purchases a separate dresser and changing table for their child's room obviously has too much free space in his home and must be looking to fill in the excess square footage.

- **Something for the Baby to Wear:** Infants grow very fast. This is a fact that escapes most purchasers of children's clothing. Any butterfly-patterned jumper or fuzzy coveralls, no matter how adorable, should be expected to have a shelf life of a few months max. Most parents are presented with more newborn clothing than they can fit into the drawers of their pastel nursery dresser, and then find that they need to purchase an entirely new wardrobe when the child hits three months and is bursting through his footie pajamas like Hulk Hogan through a tearaway muscle shirt.

  Some dads avoid the feast-famine clothing cycle by assigning certain trustworthy folks to older-age apparel duty. Having a few three-to-six, six-to-nine, or even nine-to-twelve-month outfits stuffed away in a closet for future use will be immensely helpful. Just be sure to instruct these select few people to keep the correct time of year in mind when they make their clothing selections. If your child is born in July, shorts and swimsuits sized for a six-month-old will be as useless as the newborn-sized snowsuit someone is bound to give you. "People gave us so much clothing that was seasonally inappropriate," said Stuart Z., a dad in Baltimore. "Anyone who was able to think ahead with their gifts rose so high in my esteem."

- **Someplace to Feed the Baby:** When it comes to high chairs, safe and sturdy should do the trick. Unfortunately, that may cost you, because it is frustratingly difficult to find safe, sturdy, *and* simple. Since it appears that every well-built high chair is loaded down with price-raising "bonus options," you might feel forced into purchasing a higher-end model than you originally had in mind.

Since the ones with casters tend to be slightly pricier, my wife and I figured we'd save a bit by buying a seat that didn't roll. They're all pretty lightweight, so moving one around by hand wouldn't have been a problem—and with slightly uneven hardwood floors, we saw a potential downside to wheels. After much comparison shopping, though, we had a hard time finding a stationary high chair that seemed sturdier than your average Tinkertoy construction. So we paid for the casters and had to keep them locked.

The most bewildering extra that high chair manufacturers will try to sell you on, though, is reclinability. Now, I have always been told that lying down while eating is not the best idea. So the option of letting my infant lean back while learning to take in solid food wasn't exactly a big draw. Once again, though, the nonreclining seats appeared to have been built by the first little pig. Ours had three recline positions, none of which we ever used.

One last thing about high chairs: If yours comes with toys attached, make sure the playthings can be easily removed. Getting a toddler with a finicky palate to fulfill his minimum vegetable intake is a difficult enough activity as it is; distractions in the form of a squeaking lobster and bead-filled, spring-mounted rattle do not work in your favor.

- **Someplace to Put the Baby:** Sometimes you've just got to put the kid down. My earliest memories are of being in a playpen (although I'm not sure if they're genuine recollections or images manufactured by my mind after seeing the old photos of my two-year-old self sitting in one, gnawing on the metal keys of a toy piano). The little mesh cages are still around and serve the purpose just as well as they used to, although they're now called "pla-yards." Parents felt guilty putting their baby in a "pen," but apparently they're just fine with the concept if the same three-by-two-foot enclosure is referred to as a "yard."

If you're dealing with an infant who's still in danger of rolling onto his face, though, the relatively open space afforded by a pla-yard may be too much freedom. For the youngest children, the best solution is the bouncy chair—an item which I and many of the dads I spoke to hold to be indispensable. I have yet to meet a baby who didn't love to lounge in one, and most bouncy seats come equipped with an overhead toy bar capable of stimulating and entertaining your infant long enough for you to eat dinner or maybe even solve a jumble.

When the kid is old enough to stand, you can switch to one of the larger contraptions designed for nonmobile play. They are called Activity Stations, Exersaucers, or Intellitainers, depending on who makes them, but they all essentially set your child up like the keyboardist of an eighties new wave band, putting him in a rotating seat so he can spin around and play with 360 degrees of dinging, boinging, rattling fun.

Of course, in the world of babies, there is no sure thing. You will hear, just as I did, that a baby swing is essential. We were given three. And while I know many infants who are lulled to sleep with every metronomic ride, Bryn refused to spend more than two or three minutes in one without screaming.

● **Glider Rockers:** As someone who's still a safe distance from re-tirement age, you may not have spent much time in a rocking chair in the past decade or so. But, man, have they improved.

These things are engineering marvels. They don't just sway back and forth on curved pieces of wood, they slide effortlessly along a track in a smooth arc you must feel to believe. You owe it to yourself to try one out. Just walk into any baby-goods superstore and you'll see them all lined up waiting to take your ass for a test drive. Some even come with rocking ottomans. There is a danger, though: Glider rockers are pricey, especially the top-of-the-line Dutailiers. But they're just so damn tempting. They're the high-definition flat-screen TVs of nursery furniture.

There's a ton of other stuff you'll need to get, too: bottles, car seat, monitor, bathing tub, diaper pail, and so on (not to mention strollers and carriers, which we'll tackle in Chapter 13). And with each of these purchases, you will be teased by a slew of bonus features that drive up the cost of the item and provide little or no utility. Comparison shopping is a must for the modern dad, and while we may have far more options to sort through than our parents did, we also have something they didn't have that can do most of the work for us: the Internet.

"Another thing that can really help new dads is eBay. It combines a guy's love of bidding with a chance to get really good deals and impress his wife. I bought a couple hundred dollars' worth of baby clothes for $20."

—Michael W., Paducah, KY

PARENTING PREP: Taking Classes

When it comes to prenatal education, there are two basic types of classes: the ones that prepare you for the birth itself and those that set you up for the period immediately after. Even if we're skeptical beforehand—wary that we might be investing time and money in a multiweek seminar that will provide us with just as much useful info as an hour of efficient Web surfing—we sign up anyway. We do so for the experience, because our wife wants us to, and because there's some part of us afraid to miss the one tidbit of information that will prove indispensable somewhere along the way. Invaluable life training, or six hours of your life you'll never get back? You be the judge.

New Parent Training

We'll start with the Baby Basics classes, because, frankly, there's not as much to say about them. Sometimes referred to by the unforgivably cutesy name "baby boot camps," these classes offer up the kind of rudimentary child-care knowledge that will ostensibly allow you to get through the first weeks of parenthood without having to call your mother for help.

No matter how well-read you are on parenting or how much experience you've had with young siblings or other people's babies, there are bound to be certain nuts-and-bolts elements of infant care that will be new to you (navel maintenance anyone?). One New York dad confessed to me that even though he found the diapering and feeding lessons a bit dumbed down for his tastes, learning that an infant's soft skull can be temporarily molded into a conic shape during delivery helped him avert a panic attack when his own son showed up doing a Beldar Conehead impression.

"It was nice to learn in the class that you don't need to bathe an infant every day," said Ted H. of Brooklyn. "Of course, we've taken that lesson to the extreme. Sometimes we're like, 'It's May, we should probably wash him.'"

Parenting 101 classes have another, less obvious purpose: ego boosting. These classes always seem to be filled with an inordinate number of students (and not necessarily just the dads) who repeatedly drop their crash-test dummy babies and can't seem to figure out which hole the thermometer goes in. Occasionally, you'll see some misstep so egregious (picking the baby up by its head) or hear some question so obvious ("If it's a boy, do we have to stand him up to pee?") that you'll start glancing around the room in an attempt to figure out where the hidden camera has been stashed. That surge of superiority you feel? That's your first true initiation into the culture of modern parenthood.

Birthing Lessons

While there are countless birthing techniques out there, the longtime reigning champ is the Lamaze method. Even if you take a generic no-logo birthing class, Lamaze lessons may be included in the curriculum.

If you've ever seen a sitcom with a pregnant character, you know exactly what to expect. Seriously. No surprises here. Lamaze class is one of the very few things of which Hollywood offers a consistently accurate depiction ("Our birthing class was fun only in that it was like, 'Hey, I'm in an episode of *Friends*!'" said Joe S. of Ewa Beach, Hawaii). Before you go, you can make a checklist of things to expect: Men kneeling behind their huffing-and-puffing partners; lots of floor mats; a soft-spoken, slightly new age-y instructor; and at least one guy (presumably the comic protagonist of the show you've unwittingly walked into) who seems flummoxed by the whole experience and does something totally wacky.

"Our birthing class was a little whole-earth, crunchy granola for me. There was one particular exercise where the instructor had everybody lay on the floor in a circle—the moms *and* the dads—and she began this breathing relaxation exercise. She started with, '*Breeeeeeathe* in deeply through your head, feel your head relax.' Then, 'Breathe through your neck,' 'Breathe through your shoulders,' and so on, all the way down the body, through every part you could think of. Then after about twenty minutes of this, she gets to '*Breeeeeeathe* through your vagina.' Somehow we all managed to hold it together at the time, but years later, the guys from the class can still bring it up with one another and get a guaranteed laugh."

—Bob U., New York, NY

As for the actual usefulness of the Lamaze technique, some parents insist it works wonders in the delivery room, others feel it's a placebo at best, and still more forget everything they've learned about it by the time contractions begin to hit ("The breathing part kind of went out the window as soon as my wife started pushing," said one Southern dad). My wife got nothing from Lamaze lessons other than frustration and perhaps a bit of envy over her classmates' lung capacities; she simply couldn't breathe the way the teachers told her to. All the inhaling and exhaling just succeeded in making her light-headed. Halfway through the class, we decided that the risk of my wife's breathing not being rhythmic enough during labor was preferable to her passing out on a yoga mat in the middle of the class.

One benefit of birthing instruction is that it may give you a head start on making friends with other parents. A surprising number of men I spoke to said that they and their wives hit it off with other couples they met during birthing courses. Some continue to hold regular "class reunions" long after all the babies have arrived. I guess there's something about a month and a half of panting on the floor together that can really bring people closer.

As I stated earlier, though, there's more than one way to deliver a baby. Lamaze may be a household name, but the Bradley method has a long and storied history as well. The method's creator, Dr. Robert Bradley, was one of the first major proponents of fathers in the delivery room, and the term "Bradley method" is often used interchangeably with "husband-coached childbirth." I personally think the main reason Bradley is not used as frequently is because the classes go on for three months. And the courses are that long because Bradley is *hard core*. The ultimate aim of the Bradley school is drug-free childbirth, and the road to that goal is paved with real work. Still, the few dads I spoke to who used Bradley loved it, probably because of the level of involvement it gave them in the pregnancy.

"In Bradley, you watch what the mother's eating, watch her stress level, make sure she's doing her stretching exercises," explained George R. of Austin, Texas. "I didn't go to the extremes that the class instructed me to, though. I think I would have gotten on my wife's nerves if I had."

If you're lucky enough to find a class (and it need not be one that is affiliated with any particular birthing philosophy) that will expose you to the myriad alternative birthing positions that exist, you'll be in for some of the most exciting surprises in all of prenatal education. Rare is the man worldly enough to sit through the entire roster of poses and not experience at least a few involuntary moments of eyebrow raising or impressed nodding. You have probably gone through most of your life thinking that women give birth on their backs in hospital beds with a doctor crouched between their splayed knees, and while that is still the most common scenario, it is far from the only option.

Kneeling, squatting, side-lying, leaning back into a partner's arms, sitting in a warm tub, and hanging from some kind of trapeze-like apparatus are all possible positions for laboring. And here's the kicker: All these methods have some kind of benefit over the old-fashioned lie-back-and-spread-'em pose. Standard back delivery, as your instructor will inform you with iconoclastic glee, achieved its popularity because it is the easiest position for the doctor, who can just pull up a chair and hang out down there until the baby peeks out to say hello. When the woman takes a more vertical stance—voila!—gravity takes its course and helps out quite a bit in the pushing department. After hearing all the details, you may find yourself walking out of the birthing-methods class vowing that the mother of your child will never lie down for the whims of a fascist medical community—and then, later, when your wife is delivering on her back in a hospital bed anyway, at least you'll have some righteous indignation as a helpful distraction.

BIRTH: THE MOVIE

If you have never done so before, you should see footage of a woman giving birth (unless your wife has a C-section scheduled, at which point, the whole human-popping-from-vagina image is irrelevant). Such a film will probably be screened as part of any class you may take. Even if you opt out of classes, find a way to get your hands on some video—borrow home movies from some camcorder-happy, exhibitionist friends; check the classifieds at the back of your local alternative paper. At the very least, watch one of the four hundred daily childbirth specials on the Discovery Channel or TLC (your wife may be constantly tuned in to them anyway).

There are many men—even those who are 100 percent behind being in the delivery room—who are afraid to see the movie. What I find odd is that these guys who blanch at the thought of seeing a live birth are often the same people who will sit through a George Romero film marathon and then argue with one another about which zombie's head explosion looked the most realistic. Yes, there will be some blood—but unless you've been expertly diverting your eyes once a month, you should already be somewhat familiar with that. And yes, there will also be some slime and goop, but nothing *Ghostbusters* didn't prepare you for.

Frankly, if you're too squeamish to watch the film, you're going to need to do something to try to get over it (perhaps confront your fear of icky things by playing the old Halloween party game where you stick your hand into a bowl of grapes while blindfolded and someone tells you they're really witches' eyeballs). Because the birth is far from the end of the messiness. After you take that infant home, expect to be covered in all manner of bodily excretions for the better part of a year.

Of course, no movie will adequately prepare you for the experience of seeing the birth of your own child ("It just seemed kind of clinical watching it on TV," said one dad. "It was *completely* different for the live run when you are right there in the middle of the action"). Without doubt, the actual event will be a bit overwhelming, and that's why it helps to have some level of familiarity with the visuals. Knowing ahead of time what you should expect to see will help you be able to do more during your child's birth than just gape in awe at the special effects.

D-DAY: The Delivery

One fact you must face is that men today are expected to be present when their children are born. Even sitcom dads show up for the birth (provided they aren't accidentally locked in a broom closet). In the twenty-first century, if you let your wife scream and strain through hours of grueling labor while you sit in a waiting room scribbling away at the *Yes & Know Invisible Ink Book* you picked up at the hospital gift shop, you will be considered a boorish, insensitive lout. And the current pressure on fathers to be in the delivery room has become a bone of contention for some men.

In an essay in *The New York Times* on Father's Day 2004, writer Rick Marin bemoaned living in a culture that forced him to bear witness to the blood and gore of his own child's birth and penalized him for preferring to pace in the waiting room instead. Marin described his reservations as "a combination of squeamishness and an urge to rebel against the whole 'we're pregnant' culture." He writes about how his fear of the delivery room began when he saw footage of Sting's baby being born in the 1985 documentary, *Bring On the Night,* which still "haunts [him] to this day." But one could easily get the impression that he's using the gross-out factor as a smoke screen, when he also makes comments like, "Surely the last person a woman wants relaxing her in the throes of childbirth is her husband."

Methinks the daddy doth protest too much.

"I have a weak stomach. I do not think I will watch the birth. But I will be in the room."   —Billy S., Dix, IL

I'll be blunt: I don't understand the "Why would I want to see that?" school of thought. I wanted to be there to help ease my wife through what I knew would be a painful ordeal (which she wanted, too, by the way); I wanted to be immediately accessible in the possible event of any complications; and, after nine months of anticipation, I wanted to hold my daughter in my arms at the earliest possible moment—whether she was a little slimy or not. While I can't say for sure that every father I've spoken to was gung ho about being present at the birth (I didn't ask all of them), I definitely didn't hear a single complaint about being expected to show up for the delivery. Most men now are at their partners' bedsides by choice, looking upon the opportunity as a privilege—one that was not readily available only a few decades ago.

However, if you are considering sitting out the birth, that's your prerogative. It's safe to say that whether or not a man is physically present to cut the umbilical cord speaks nothing of his ability to parent a child; after all, there are many new fathers who end up being unavailable for the birth through no fault of their own (unexpectedly short labor, car breakdown on the way to the hospital, narcolepsy). But if you are not one of the guys who plan to carpe that particular diem, please, read on anyway, so you'll at least know what you're missing.

A. Gentlemen, Take Your Positions: Your Relevance During Labor

No matter how much planning you've done, no matter how many classes you've attended, you'll never know how your labor and delivery experience is going to go down until it happens. Men often have to fight to balance their jittery desire to help their partners and the sneaking suspicion that they are really of no more practical use than the fern in the corner of the hospital room. Should you find yourself in this situation, the emotionally and physically depleted woman lying before you will probably leave you awestruck by the levels of sheer strength, stamina, and willpower she demonstrates while enduring hours of painful contractions and straining every muscle in her body to perform what appears to the naked eye to be a physiologically impossible feat. She will become Supergirl, the Bionic Woman, and all three original Charlie's Angels rolled into one—while you spend the majority of your time fetching her a cup of ice chips to suck on.

Throughout these trying moments, keep in mind that these are your last few hours as Expectant Father, and that very soon, after you drop the modifier, the importance of your role will be boundless.

In fact, there is plenty for you to do in the delivery room. In the earlier stages of labor, you can play masseur, soothing her through the agony of her contractions; or bodyguard, policing the bedside manner of the various medical personnel who pop in and out of the room and interceding whenever that one disgruntled nurse shows her face. You can usurp the role of the call button, running out into the hallway to forcibly grab an unsuspecting orderly each time the ice supply runs low. And while many men are not happy about being relegated to the position of pep squad leader, encouragement and moral support are the most obvious ways in which you can help your wife during her labor (and honestly, toward the end, you'll probably reach a point where you're just so damn impressed by her, you'll want to cheer like one of the extras at the feel-good climax of *Rudy*). Then, during those final stages of pushing, you can grasp your wife's hand and huff, "Breathe, baby, breathe! You can do it!" (though, should you actually do this, you're likely to annoy her within about thirty seconds).

Of course, you can also play documentarian. "Before the due date, get all the film you will need, all the batteries, and charge any and all camcorder batteries. Even if they won't let you film the birth, it's nice to get pictures as soon as possible," advises Shannon F. of Chesapeake, Virginia. "My wife had a C-section, so they wouldn't allow me to record the birth, but as soon as they got the baby to the table to clean him off, they let me come over and start snapping away. I looked like a lost tourist. I had two digital cameras, a 35mm, one VHS camcorder, and one minidigital camcorder. I was *so* worried that one would break down."

B. Enter the Doula:
Fighting That Third-Wheel Feeling

Doulas, for those of you not aware, are professional childbirth assistants, hired to offer emotional and informational support throughout the pregnancy, delivery, and beyond—and they're becoming an increasingly common presence at childbirths. They can, and often may be expected to, perform many of the duties listed in the section above. It's understandable that expectant dads might feel compelled to compete with the doula for responsibility in the delivery room. But in that high-pressure setting, time and energy cannot be wasted on trying to depose the doula. These specialists are meant to help the dad out, too (it's in their job description), so the smart man will take a step back and let the doula handle some of the (literal) grunt work.

"It was my wife's choice to have a doula, and I was a little resistant at first," said Peter R. of New York City. "It was male instinct: If you're here then why am I here? I went along with it because I knew it would make my wife more comfortable. When my wife first went into labor, I was busy timing the contractions and talking her through them; then the doula showed up with all sorts of better advice. And in the end, I was glad she was there. She did things I never would have thought of doing. She mooed. My wife was moaning, and the doula made these mooing noises with her, and that helped calm my wife. I certainly wouldn't have ever thought of mooing. It's natural for guys to want to be the fixer, and not a lot of guys think of comforting and hair-stroking as being active. But the bottom line with a doula is experience; this is someone who coaches births for a living. I felt a little displaced, but I just had to suck it up. When all was said and done, I wouldn't change it."

You could also be stricken by performance anxiety when it comes time for you to do your part as labor assistant in front of a person whose expertise in the area obviously trumps yours. Imagine the stage fright that could set in when the woman who has been soothing away your wife's cramps with stunningly effective pressure-point massage, asks you to step in and take over for a while. It's like having Jasper Johns step away from a canvas, hand you a brush, and say, "Go ahead; now *you* paint an American flag."

If either unhealthy competitiveness or fear of failure should set in, remember: The doula is not your enemy. She is your Obi-Wan Kenobi; watch her, learn from her—do not turn to the Dark Side.

C. Hit Me With Your Best Shot: Daddy's Labor Pain

Doula or no doula, there's one job that can *only* be taken on by the father of the baby, and that is Human Punching Bag. While in the throes of agony, the desire to smash one's fists into something soft and fleshy is human nature. Even in her most severe moments of pain, your wife would probably restrain her impulse to land an uppercut into the jaw of her obstetrician. You, however, can boldly offer yourself up to her as the human equivalent of those sticks that Navy SEALs clamp their teeth down onto while their commanding officer sets their broken legs after parachuting mishaps in the jungle. Perhaps there's even something cathartic in it for you, a chance to share the pain a little bit. As my wife repeatedly punched my arm, pulled my hair, and even bit my hand, I couldn't help but think of Bill Cosby's old stand-up routine where he described his wife demonstrating the pain of childbirth for him by pulling his lower lip up over his head. After it was all over, my wife was completely shocked when I later rolled up my sleeves, revealing the bruises that dotted my right arm (she didn't even remember doing it), and friends to whom I showed off the damage were impressed enough to dole a little token pity in my direction.

One must also keep in mind that this timeworn scenario of the long, grueling birthing process is, again, only one of several possibilities. Despite the plethora of horror tales you might hear, easy labors are not all that rare. (I spoke to one man who accompanied his wife to her bed, popped into the bathroom to wash up, and stepped back out to find her already cradling their newborn daughter.) For a new dad, there might even be some disappointment in a labor that is too short and makes for no good stories to tell later on; just don't share that with your wife.

> "We put so much time and thought into the pregnancy. We went through endless hours of planning for the labor, we took classes, we spent money on doulas, and then when it happened, it was over in a blink. There was one really rough hour there for my wife, but when it was over, I was like, 'That's it?' The birth wasn't chapter one; it wasn't even the introduction or the preface; it was the copyright page."
>
> —Bill T., Brooklyn, NY

Obviously, there can also be a big difference in pain level for the mom depending upon whether or not drugs are used. A woman who has had an epidural administered is a lot less likely to turn into Jake La Motta on you, despite the fact that she's still pushing an entire human being through a 10-centimeter orifice. Conversely, if for any reason, labor needs to be induced (through an injection of the synthetic hormone Pitocin), the contractions are reportedly more painful than they are during the birth of the average "I'll come out when I'm good and ready" baby. If you see the inducement syringes come out, start strapping on your Kevlar.

D. C-Sections:
The Other Kind of Delivery

Twenty-eight percent of all American babies are born by Cesarean delivery. If this is the case for your wife, there truly isn't much more you can offer than hand-holding and soft words (since meandering around the OR and tinkering with the instruments would likely get you bounced out of the building). But in a situation as potentially nerve-racking for your wife as waking vivisection, that particular type of aid may be more necessary than ever.

"I peeked around the curtain a couple of times," said one Texas dad, whose wife was forced to have an emergency C-section after having planned for a natural home birth. "Whenever I got a little queasy, I would just turn back to my wife and focus on her and talk to her. A view inside your wife's abdomen—that's more than any guy really needs to see. Plus they were using a laser to cauterize the incisions, so you also had the odor of burning flesh. Let me tell you, that's a really nice smell. But I had planned to coach my wife and that meant comforting her through all of it."

Many men point out that, in a way, Cesareans can allow a greater chance for the couple to share the birthing process, as both of you become nervous spectators waiting together for the Great Oz behind the curtain to pop up for the big reveal.

"When they told my wife she needed a C-section, her response was great. Rather than view it as a failure of her ability to have the child naturally—or as the oppression of a dehumanizing hospital system—she just said, 'If it's best for the baby, let's do

it.' Her answer deflated my own panicked indignation and re-minded me that the baby, not the delivery experience, was most important."
                                          —Kevin K., Perth, Australia

E. . . . And Baby Makes Thirty-Seven: The Crowd Scene

The actual moment of your child's birth may be one of the most sur-real events you ever witness. And not just in the ways you might think. Yes, seeing the baby emerge from the womb is quite a sight to behold, but at least you're expecting that to happen. You may not be prepared for the sudden influx of strangers into the room. Through-out the entire labor process, the cast may be a relatively small en-semble. At the moment of delivery, though, seemingly dozens of other people may burst in through the door with Keystone Kops fre-neticism: extra nurses, orderlies, note-taking medical students, a lactation consultant, someone from the cord blood bank, clipboard-toting record-keepers, moppers, perhaps a documentary film crew. With the spontaneous appearance of the crowd, you may start hal-lucinating balloons and confetti falling from the ceiling as if you've just won a prize for being the One Millionth Shopper; only instead of being presented with an oversize cardboard check, somebody hands you an infant. And it seems like the longer the labor lasts, the more people show up at the end. This is probably done for your ben-efit, just to give it all an extra-exciting finish in case you've started to grow bored with the monotony of several hours' worth of "breathe-push-breathe-push." It does make you want to seriously consider home birth, though.

F. _____ at First Sight:
The End of the Beginning

There is no way to predict exactly what you will feel upon seeing your child for the first time. So there's no real need to waste time and energy wondering whether your individual reaction was correct or appropriate. But lots of guys do. Thanks to popular wisdom and stories we've heard from other parents (many probably apocryphal), we have been led to believe that we should experience some sort of miracle snap-bonding, an instant and overwhelming love connection that overtakes us on first glimpse of a waxy, mottled newborn child. If this magic trick doesn't happen right away, it's all too easy for doubts to start creeping into a man's mind about his readiness or ability to be a good parent. But this is a case where first impressions do not count.

> "After I first found out my wife was pregnant, I felt scared. I felt a knot in my stomach, thinking about the grave responsibility of being a father, with all the financial implications, the sense of a loss of freedom. When the day came, though, the baby's health was in jeopardy, and it was the most stressful event in my life. When it was over, I was just so glad that baby and mommy were doing well, that, honestly, none of those initial worries even entered my mind again."
>
> —Mark S., Chicago, IL

Here are just a few of the many varied reactions men have admitted to upon first seeing their children: fear, weeping, "Which one of us does he look like?," instant paranoia, momentary amnesia, *"Woohoo!,"* weak legs, a need to sit down, "I hope that red mark goes away," cotton mouth, panic, relief, "Can I do this?," "Now what?," pride, joy, numbness. That last one was me: As my daughter popped out, the first thing I did was yell, "It's a girl," and then, about three seconds later, I got a case of full-body pins-and-needles. It stuck with me as I watched the nurses carry Bryn to the corner of the room to get her vital stats, and vanished only when they asked me if I wanted to hold her.

Your emotions in those first moments are likely to be extremely mixed. And they may change often over the next few hours, or even the following few days. In time, though, you will come to love that child in a way you never thought possible. You may question that love a few months down the road when you're attempting a half-asleep 3 a.m. diaper change and the wailing kid pees on you. But we'll worry about that later.

PART II

HEY, THIS IS DIFFERENT: THE TRANSITION

All right, pregnancy's over; forget the last nine months and let's move on.

You're going to be living in a whole new universe from here on—one filled with playdates, Muppets, and hovering grandparents. But you can't even think about taking on such challenges before you adjust to your immediate surroundings. From the moment you carry that baby across the threshold, the smallest elements of your daily life will be transformed. So before we head out into the world with baby in hand, let's first explore the changes, large and small, that will take place closer to home.

CHAPTER 4

Nuclear Testing: How Dad, Mom, and Baby Find a Rhythm as a New Family

In the early months of parenthood, it can be difficult to hang on to any semblance of your former life. You will be tired: Newborns can sleep sixteen to twenty hours a day, yet somehow manage to keep you from getting more than three or four hours. You will be harried: While tending to baby's constant demands, your daily schedule will become one massive improv act. You will be increasingly on edge: Living with a soundtrack of frequent bawling will tax your nerves and make it nearly impossible to think clearly. You might also feel jealous (of the early mother-baby bond), cramped (by well-meaning, but intrusive visitors), and defensive (due to being snapped at by a spouse who is just as brain-addled as you are—if not more so). And to be honest, the child will be far more work than fun in the beginning. In all likelihood, your infant will inspire hair-pulling fits of frustration just as often as he'll inspire fawning and doting.

It has often been noted that there's an evolutionary benefit to the fact that babies come out looking so darn cute. The only problem with this theory is that newborns aren't always all that attractive. By two or three months old, sure, they're adorable—but before that, they can be wrinkly, lumpy, grayish creatures. More E.T. than Swee'Pea.

The beginning is rough, but it won't last forever. Before long, you'll have a lot more to worry about than wondering where the crusty stub of your infant's umbilical went when it dried up and fell off, or whether your wife's supply of nipple cream is running low. For now, take a vacation from decorum; why not savor the primal chaos that ensues once a baby comes into the picture? The first few months of parenthood are the only time in your postbachelor life that you'll have complete freedom to be as much of a slob as you want. Lack of sleep will have you running on pure adrenaline, which can go to your head like a strong whiskey and fill you with a nice sense of invincibility ("Did I just slam a door on my foot? I care not! I will limp onward to fetch my crying child!"). And you'll prove wrong anybody who has ever called child care a feminine task: How can you not feel manly when you have an exhausted wife and a tiny, utterly helpless infant relying on you for care? You are that ultimate masculine archetype, The Hunter (even if what you're hunting for is a misplaced pacifier).

THREE IS A MAGIC NUMBER: Meet Your New Roommate

Perhaps you and your wife have spent months, maybe years, perfecting a morning routine so efficient it makes the ghost of Henry Ford shake his fist with envy. The alarm goes off at 7:00. You brew the coffee while she jumps in the shower. You switch places with her, and she's got bowls of cereal poured for you both by the time you're dried off. You each take turns brushing your teeth while the other gets dressed. And you're out the door by 8:00.

Now let's add a newborn infant into that scenario.

The alarm goes off at 7:00. You were already up six times during the night, so you hit snooze—but the child's wailing drags you out of bed anyway. You fetch him from the bassinet, and while your bleary-eyed wife nurses him, you shuffle into the kitchen to start the coffee—stubbing your big toe on the bouncy chair along the way—only to remember that you've been out of coffee for three days. Your wife calls: The baby is latched to her breast, but she urgently needs to pee. She hands you your son and dashes away. You pace the hallways, trying to calm the unhappy child until Mommy returns. Once she's back, you quickly shower, but there's no time to shave, because it's already 7:38 (Note: There's no better time to grow a beard than the first few days after having a baby). While your wife washes up, you take the baby back and sift through your shirts to find one free of spit-up stains. After she returns, the two of you juggle the infant back and forth as you both get dressed: shirt, baby, socks, baby, pants, baby. Then a deep inhale lets you know it's time for a diaper change. As you fumble one-handed with a still-shrink-wrapped box of wipes, you glance at the clock. It's 8:00. You're exhausted, starving, running late, and since you haven't gotten to brush your teeth, you suddenly realize your mouth tastes like a used insole.

Have you and your wife suddenly become bumbling oafs? No—you're the same capable people you were before. So who *is* the troublemaker here? That's right: the baby. See, the problem is not just that you've got another individual living with you; it's that your new roommate is not pulling his own (admittedly light) weight. Newborns lead a very feral life in the beginning—it's all eating, sleeping, excreting. Your part is to provide the sustenance, put them to bed, and clean up the crap. If you've ever played *The Sims*—where you have to make sure your character's hunger, rest, and bathroom meters never dip too low—you should be pretty familiar with the rules of the baby-keeping game.

Whereas the art of give-and-take has allowed you and your wife to coexist—you've agreed to ignore all your pen caps that have become misshapen by teeth marks; in exchange, she'll just hum quietly to herself when you chew too loudly—infants know no compromise. The baby can't say, "Okay, if you put a little ointment on that diaper rash down there, I've got dinner covered tonight." Adults need to give and give and give, without expecting anything from the child in return.

That may sound obvious, but there are plenty of guys (and women, too) who are a bit shocked to discover they're not even getting *emotional* payback. "I found it really difficult in the beginning," one dad admitted. "I knew it would be a lot of hard work, but stupidly, I was thinking I'd also be playing with the baby right away. Yeah, *that* happened."

"In the first few months, sometimes all you want is a smile, and instead you just get that dead stare," said Chris F. of Las Vegas. "I honestly wasn't prepared for that."

There's a real danger of hard feelings developing if your wife appears to be getting more out of her relationship with the baby than you are. "For the first three or four months, my son just wouldn't respond to me at all," said one New York dad. "It was frustrating. I couldn't bathe him, put him to sleep, or feed him without him crying. He insisted on having his mother, and he would let her do anything. I felt awful. I'd just keep telling myself, it *has* to get better later on." FYI: This dad and his now three-year-old son have since become virtually inseparable.

Before you start looking at your infant as a twenty-inch taskmaster, it helps to remember that the payoff is on the way—just a few months down the road. In the meantime, you do what you must. That could mean accepting household changes that happen organically (the overall neatness level of the household will automatically default to that of the person who had the more lenient prebaby definition of "clutter"). Or it may require actively working to adapt your own behavior to the new situation—if, say, you're the type of guy who likes to sleep diagonally, cramping your partner into a pizza-box-sized corner of the bed, and suddenly a suckling infant has found his way in between the two of you. Think of this period as a lesson in delayed gratification.

> "The first six months were incredibly hard. For the majority of the time that the baby was awake, she was attached to my wife's breast. And she was a rough sleeper, so putting her to bed was no joy. After six months, though, things began to change— suddenly, she was a little person. From that point on, things got a lot more fun really fast." —Bob U., Brooklyn, NY

THE ART OF WAR: Arguing in Front of a Baby

> "My wife and I alternate pissy moods. We'll say to each other, 'Okay, it's your day to be irritable.'" —John P., New York, NY

In the turbulence of the first few months, short tempers are to be expected. Even if you and your wife rarely fight, a spat over which of you put the empty wipes container back on the changing table is somewhere around the bend. What can come as a shock is the change, not just in what you argue about, but in *how* you argue. I heard about one couple whose prebaby spats were all-out scream-fests (the kind that made throw pillows live up to their name). Since becoming parents, these same two people now possess the ability to have a discussion that is pointed, but in such an even-tempered manner that a bystander who didn't speak English might think they were debating ranch dressing versus Thousand Island.

Of course, this transformation doesn't happen without work

(don't go slapping a "World's Tiniest Marriage Counselor" T-shirt on your baby just yet). When arguing in front of a baby, you can—in the parlance of *Highlights for Children*—be a Goofus or a Gallant. Compiled from the expertise of dads all across the country, here are some guidelines for carrying on a more dignified war of words.

The Rules of Engagement

1. **Do not put off the fight.** Many of the men I spoke with described their attempts to hold off on any heated exchanges in the baby's presence. While such intentions are noble, if you're postponing arguments you're doing yourself a disservice. Yes, infants are powerful empaths who suck up negative vibes like a DustBuster on Cheerio crumbs. So even if your words are as meaningless to a baby as the dog-nabbit, rassa-frassin' expletives of a Yosemite Sam rant, the anger behind them may come through loud and clear. But when the long-awaited peace of your infant's nap time comes, the last thing you want to do is spend it rehashing some issue from earlier in the day that you've already forgotten but your wife hasn't. As one dad said to me, "Men might be able to let a problem slip straight out of their minds, but women can easily start an argument with, 'Remember last week . . .' " When the majority of your day is spent careening from one baby-related chore to another, the child's nap time is like a slice of nirvana; immediately dispensing with any harsh feelings is even more important for parents than for a childless couple.

Goofus:

WIFE: We need to talk.
YOU: Not in front of the baby.

Gallant:

WIFE: We need to talk.

YOU: All right, let's do this now, because I plan to be snoring five minutes after the kid goes down.

2. **Get to the point *fast*.** Since your child can interrupt you at any moment, the ability to argue efficiently is a vital skill. Without it, you're likely to stir up all sorts of anger and then have to leave it hanging without resolution if the baby starts crying. "You discover the beauty of brevity," said Paul E. of Chicago. "My wife and I learned to argue in bullet points."

Goofus:

YOU: I can't believe this happened again. You know, I tried to let it slide the first few times, but I just can't anymore. This is one thing you always do that really, really gets to me, and if it doesn't stop, it's going to—[Baby screams: *"WAAAAAAAAHHHHHH!"*]. Oh, crap.

Gallant:

YOU: Please stop wiping up baby drool with my socks.

3. **Argue at a moderate volume.** Say whatever you want, but do so in softer voices and more measured tones. Not only will this keep you from upsetting the baby, but fights that don't involve escalating decibel levels generally involve more thinking—always a good thing.

Goofus:

YOU: DAMN IT, YOU LEFT THE BABY MONITOR ON ALL DAY AND NOW THE BATTERIES ARE DEAD!

WIFE: WELL, IF YOU'D BOUGHT MORE BATTERIES TO BEGIN WITH, LIKE I SAID YOU SHOULD, IT WOULDN'T BE A PROBLEM!

Gallant:

YOU: You left the baby monitor on all day and now the batteries are dead.

WIFE: Actually, honey, wasn't that up to you? You got him out of bed this morning.

YOU: Did I? Oh, yeah. Sorry.

4. **Use code words.** This one may not be essential in the very beginning, but sooner than you think, your baby will be able to recognize certain key words and phrases ("car," "nap," "kitty," etc.). Avoiding those verbal triggers is a good habit to get into. If an argument centers around something the baby either wants or fears (like food or vaccine shots, respectively), you need to state your case without speaking any of the forbidden terms, as if you were playing a game of Taboo. Aside from keeping the kid in the dark, this method of arguing can make whatever you're incensed about feel too silly to take seriously.

Goofus:

YOU: You left dirty bottles in the sink overnight and now they're all crusted with dried formula. [Baby starts crying for his liquid breakfast.]

Gallant:

YOU: You left dirty . . . nipple-topped beverage units in the sink overnight and now they're all crusted with . . . a whitish vitamin-enriched liquid. [Baby remains focused on sucking his toes.]

5. **Pay attention to the baby.** Parents who ignore their child in favor of arguing with each other will only have more therapy bills to foot later on. But in addition to that rather obvious point, you should keep your eyes on the kid because, well, babies are cute. Come on, how are you going to stay angry when you spot an adorable chubby-cheeked cherub grinning up at you?

Goofus:

YOU: [Focusing only on your spouse] You can be such an unbelievable . . . !

Gallant:

YOU: [Focusing on your spouse] You can be such an unbelievable . . . [Switching focus to the baby] . . . Aw, what am I so angry about?

BOY WONDER: Which Parent Is the Sidekick?

All new parents doubt their abilities at some point (okay, many points), but too many guys defer to their partners on all things baby in the belief that mothers will inherently know what to do. I'm not quite sure why so many guys—including those of us who plan to be very active fathers—still fall into this line of thinking. Perhaps it's because women often have more babysitting experience from youth; maybe it's an assumption that their moms passed on all sorts of confidential info to them; or maybe it's because we've spent our lives hearing women brag about having a "maternal instinct." And while there is something to be said for such instinct, gender alone does not impart factual knowledge about parenting. Your wife's ovaries aren't little anatomical Cyrano de Bergeracs, whispering internally and giving her all the winning lines. She's just as capable of being incompetent with kids as you, and thinking otherwise may put undue pressure on her to be Supermom (trust me, she'll get quite enough of that from other people over the next eighteen years). I remember being a bit taken aback when my wife was pacing our apartment trying to calm down a colicky three-week-old Bryn, and finally passed her off to me, saying, "You try something." That's when I discovered that my left shoulder turned out to be a miracle pillow for our newborn daughter. My wife was relieved and I felt the first stirrings of fatherly pride.

> "I think at the beginning I was afraid I knew less about what I was doing than my wife did. Luckily, I am married to a wise woman who realized that I needed to get over those fears—and that she needed to help me get over them by not doing everything herself. For example, my first attempts at bathing the baby were a screaming nightmare, while hers went calmly and peacefully. I thought perhaps she should be the sole bather— but she made me get back on the horse again. Now everything is fine."   —Jeff M., Takoma Park, MD

Assuming your wife doesn't want to lay claim to every child-related task herself, there are two distinctly different paths you and she can take toward coparenting:

Share Everything:

Core Tenet: Take turns—Mom and Dad alternate duty on all parenting tasks.

Motto: "I suctioned her nose last time."

Pros: Knowing there will be at least some diapers you don't need to change, some handprints you don't need to scrub off walls, and some flailing tantrums during which you won't need to fear an accidental kick to the groin.

Cons: Scrutiny and competition—when you're muttering to yourself, "Wow, I am *so* much neater with the spoon-feeding than she is," or "Why do her hands *never* smell like Desitin?"

Strict Division of Labor:

Basic Tenet: Each parent has his or her own designated responsibilities.

Motto: "You put it in one end, I deal with it when it comes out the other."

Pros: A chance to perfect your chosen duties. Ask any expert. Children love routine the way VH1 loves countdowns.

Cons: Job jealousy—when it occurs to you one night while scrubbing congealed rice cereal residue off the high chair that your wife, currently bathing the baby amid pink suds and rubber ducks, totally got the better deal on this one.

As usual, a blend of the two often works best. (The only places in life where it's generally preferable to go with the "extreme" are alt-sports video games and Gatorade flavors.) And, of course, there will be certain tasks that almost always work better as two-person jobs, as well as those that must be performed by one specific parent. Take, for instance, breast-feeding.

NURSING A GRUDGE: Breast-feeding—
With or Without You

We men have been cursed with nipples that have as much actual function as the flashing lights on the control panels of the starship *Enterprise*. No milk production means no breast-feeding. Nursing is a mommy job.

Your wife may pump and store some of her breast milk, which will increase your ability to feed your child in the early months, but no bottle—no matter how expensive or highly rated on Epinions— will make you feel equal. It's a commonly held belief that the mother-child bond begins with breast-feeding. That's why, even as women complain to us over and over again about monotony, soreness, and cracked areolae, even the manliest among us may suddenly find himself daydreaming about, well, having teats.

"It would make me crazy that my daughter would be crying and there was nothing I could do about it other than hand her off to my wife—who could soothe her immediately by breast-feeding," said Jeff R. of Chicago.

Fret not, you *can* insinuate yourself into the breast-feeding picture. One of the simplest things you can do to assist your wife at feeding time is to bring the baby to her. When the kid lets loose with an "I'm hungry" cry (which, in time, you will learn to distinguish from the "I'm sleepy" cry and the "I'm afraid of Snuffleupagus" cry), take some of the burden off your spouse by transporting the infant to her for meal time. Yes, this pretty much makes you the designated driver for breast-feeding. But think about it from the child's point of view: She needs nourishment, she calls out; Daddy appears before her to take her to what she needs. Sure, Mom is the one producing the food, but the baby begins to associate Daddy's appearance with the eventual intake of sweet, sweet milk. When you take someone out to dinner, who does that person thank? You or the chef? There you have it: bonding.

You can also be there to comfort your wife, especially if she's having difficulty nursing. The process doesn't come easily to a lot of women; their breasts hurt, they can't produce enough milk, or the baby won't latch on correctly. Your spouse can grow frustrated and perhaps even think she's a failure. That's where she needs you—to remind her not to beat herself up over any difficulties she has, and to run interference against the assholes who will try to make her feel like a bad mother if she has to bottle-feed.

Babies do like bottle feedings, too. Which is why we men shouldn't turn our noses up at those opportunities, either. As soon as screw-on tops enter the picture, it's Daddy's time to shine.

> "I was really jealous that I couldn't breast-feed. So I wrestled with my son instead; or I'd be the guy who threw him in the air and made him laugh. That was my way of breast-feeding."
> —Andrew B., Milwaukee, WI

EXIT SANDMAN: Sleep Deprivation and You

Whatever sleeping arrangements you've decided on initially (a bassinet in the corner of your room, a crib in the baby's own room, a three-sided "co-sleeper" that attaches to the side of your bed, or an invitation for Junior to share your Sealy Posturepedic), frequent night feedings in the first few months will ensure plenty of un-wanted wake-up calls. Consider yourself blessed with a miracle baby if your child starts sleeping through the night as soon as she comes home from the hospital (a few of the dads I spoke to said their kids did—but another guy I interviewed, upon learning of those claims, responded with, "What a bunch of frickin' liars!").

Parents of problem sleepers (yours truly included) can get a bit irked by hearing about hibernating newborns. I'm not saying that it's impossible for a two-week-old infant to go down for eight hours at a stretch—nor would I ever insinuate that any of the men who generously contributed their stories for this book were "frickin' liars"—but that's certainly not the norm. In some cases, there may actually just be a discrepancy in people's definitions of "sleeping through the night." When Bryn reached the point where she was waking up only three or four times over the course of a night, as opposed to ten or twelve, my wife and I were so excited by the development that we started telling people our daughter was "sleeping through the night." Then when Bryn later started going to bed and staying asleep until morning, it struck us that we had been a bit premature in our victory celebration.

So in the beginning, whether your infant wakes you four times a night or twenty times, you *will* suffer from sleep deprivation. It's just a question of how badly you'll get hit by it. "Sometimes I had to take a pillow to work and take a catnap under my desk," admits one dad.

"I have seen every possible position the hands of a clock could be in—including some that no one should have to see, like 2:11 a.m. or 4:25 a.m. I have enough memories of watching the sunrise while holding my son to last a lifetime. The first four months after the birth, I maybe had two to three hours of sleep a night and went to work in a daze sometimes."

—Eric S., Atlanta, GA

If you want to avoid stumbling through your day with all the energy of Tor Johnson in *Plan 9 from Outer Space,* the two most common suggestions I heard from dads are—prepare to have your mind blown—naps and caffeine. The former basically means giving in to your drowsiness, the latter fighting it. I've never been a good napper, so I staked my daily usefulness on the power of Colombian dark roast. (Another dad I interviewed sang the praises of green tea, "not so much for its antioxidant properties, but more because it provides a kick without making me uncontrollably wired.") For other men, sleeping whenever the baby sleeps is a biological command: "During the day, as long as you're active and engaged in what you're doing, adrenaline kicks in and you can just keep going," said Lee W. of Brooklyn. "It's when you stop that you suddenly get really, really sleepy."

To help his situation, Alex P., a dad in Palo Alto, California, made a deal with his wife. "We have strict rules about me getting up early with the kids on odd-numbered days, and her getting up if it's an even-numbered day," he said. "Otherwise, it's too easy to get into groggy, yet pointed discussions about which of us deserves to sleep in."

Preventing sluggishness is only one reason to combat sleep deprivation. Too little sleep can bring out an ugly side of you that you'd probably rather not see, and perhaps didn't even know you had. One dad I spoke to called it "The Evil." "I feel terrible even talking about it," he said, "but it's what hits you in the middle of the night when the kid's been crying for hours. You've fed him, burped him, changed him, rocked him—there's literally nothing else you can do, and he's still screaming his lungs out. That's when really horrible thoughts run through your head. And when it happens, you hate yourself for feeling it."

If you can manage to take care of a baby and never let your internal monologue lapse into a string of obscenities, please try not to blind the rest of us with the brilliance of your saintly aura. Frustration is a very human trait. And as a good father, even when you're yelling at your baby in your mind ("SHUT UP! SHUT UP! SHUT UP!"), what you're probably going to do is pick that infant up, cradle her against your shoulder, and attempt to gently rock her back to sleep.

On a happier note, you will at some point get to sleep again. Whenever it happens, it will be a joyous occasion. I can clearly remember the morning that I woke, not to a baby's cries, but to my wife's whispered shouts of "It's light out! Honey, look, it's light out!" I opened my eyes to see that she was indeed correct; the sun was shining. We had gone to bed, and not woken up again until the next morning. When Bryn started making noise a few minutes later, we practically danced out of our bedroom together to go see her.

I want to note that sometimes you can't blame the kid for your sleep deprivation. While most mothers will drop off at any opportunity, there are lots of fathers who value their guilty pleasures enough to forgo much-needed rest in favor of, say, late-night reruns of *Iron Chef*. "By the time the kids are down, I want my chance to do stuff— even stupid stuff like watching TV or playing video games," said Eric H. of Mechanicsville, Virginia (a self-proclaimed night owl). "I'll keep looking over at the clock and thinking to myself, 'Okay, if I go to bed now, I can still get four hours of sleep.'"

Though that's exactly the kind of thing that sends scientists at the National Sleep Foundation into conniptions, I cannot condemn such behavior. Since Bryn was a terrible sleeper early on, I'd often tell myself, "Why should I even try to go to bed yet? She's going to wake up in an hour anyway." Besides, cutting short your sleep time may be a necessary evil in keeping up with your prefatherhood pursuits—whether that means waking up early for a workout, staying up late to study for the LSAT, or even something slightly less honorable. Though I often regretted it in the morning, I was pleased with the fact that I got to see an entire TiVo-recorded season of *The Amazing Race* by ignoring my body's cues.

"Sleep is for pussies."—A dad in Virginia

VISITING HOURS: The Pros and Cons of Postpartum Houseguests

In the days and weeks after the birth of your child, you may be besieged by visitors. Many will drop off flowers for your wife, pat the baby on the head, and leave. Some will endear themselves to you for all time by showing up with bagloads of supermarket and drugstore supplies, knowing that you will likely be housebound for the next several days. And a few may offer to stay with you for a week or two and help you get adjusted. As appealing as it may initially seem to have a visiting-nurse/nanny on hand, make sure you ask yourself a few important questions before you pull out the AeroBed. Does your mother plan to take up some of the cooking and cleaning while you and your wife learn the ropes of parenthood, or will all the chores still fall to you while she gets in some cuddle time with her new grandchild? Is she able to give you and your wife space when you need it, or will you be feeling that four's a crowd by the second hour of her visit? Will her presence in the house make for convenient access when those inevitable "Mom, what do I do now?" moments crop up, or will it mean she constantly hovers and intercedes?

The guys I spoke to expressed almost universal appreciation for relatives who became live-in help for a few weeks. However, many of them also said they wished that their mothers (or mothers-in-law) had started their tour of duty a little later on, rather than Day One. These men said they would have liked some time for mom, dad, and baby to get used to one another without a houseguest.

It might not be a bad idea to ask any potential live-in helpers to wait, not just to allow you and your new family some solo adjustment time, but also because, frankly, the first two or three days may be easier than those that come shortly after. My wife and I were lulled into a false sense of security by a newborn who barely made a peep for the first seventy-two hours, only to discover the true power of her lung capacity on Day Four.

Be leery of any offer to drop by and "help out" for a few days that comes from a person whom you don't see all that often, though. Should this happen, give that gift horse a good flossing before you accept. Consider the following anecdote inspired by true events: Your second cousin, LuAnn from San Antonio, calls up and says, "Congratulations on the baby! You guys could probably use a little extra help right now; why don't I come by and stay for a week or two?" You're stunned by the compassionate nature of this relative whom you never would have thought had it in her to offer her services, but you give her the benefit of the doubt. Soon you find yourself struggling to adjust to life with a new infant while your lugubrious cousin—whom you later discover was only looking for an excuse to escape her own miserable husband and kids for a while—spends a week on your couch watching *The Young and the Restless,* occasionally tickling the baby, and asking, "So what are we having for dinner tonight?"

OFF THE CHARTS: Milestone Madness

Let me state this as clearly as I can: Babies develop at different rates. This is a crucial piece of information that is too often forgotten by new parents. And that can lead to all sorts of hand-wringing when you get a look at any (or worse, many) of the myriad developmental charts that are sprinkled throughout parenting literature. Your wife might even subscribe to the "What Your Baby Should Be Doing This Week" e-mail newsletter from some Web site, resulting in her calling out to you while at the computer, "Is she flapping her arms like a bird yet? She's supposed to be able to flap her arms like a bird. See if you can get her to flap!"

"I wish I'd never seen a single milestone chart," one dad told me, echoing a common sentiment.

Most dads approach developmental charts out of anticipation rather than some kind of obsessive fear that something might be wrong with their children. But even if you first grab a chart, thinking, "*Ooh,* let me see what my son's going to be doing next!" once you've seen the various baby stunts on the list lined up next to very specific ages, it's too late. If your kid diverges from the chart, the seed of anxiety is planted.

And the chance that your child won't be hitting all the marks is pretty damn high, considering the remarkable level of specificity with which these charts are written. Take some of these examples pulled from the *What to Expect When You're Expecting* sequel, *What to Expect the First Year.*

Your baby should be able to:

- by 2 months, respond to a bell
- by 2½ months, follow an object in an arc about six inches above the face past the midline
- by 3⅔ months, laugh out loud
- by 5 months, pay attention to a raisin

And then the reader is advised: "If your baby seems not to have reached one or more of these milestones, check with the doctor."

With this kind of detail, these charts seem impossible to misinterpret. Who can blame an inexperienced parent for running off to the pediatrician, shouting, "Oh my God, my baby pays no attention to raisins whatsoever!"

You're never going to see a developmental chart carrying a "For Entertainment Purposes Only" label. So before you spend the time doing the math to figure out exactly when it is that your baby turns 3⅔ months old, read the fine print to remind yourself that the data they use is based on averages—a fact that also means you shouldn't get a swelled head if your one-month-old is responding to bells ahead of schedule. I remember when Bryn started stacking blocks at about nine months old, way earlier than the twelve-month target given by many charts. My wife and I were high-fiving each other in celebration of having produced a prodigy. Later, when Bryn was several months behind the average in walking, well, at least I still had the memories of those blocks.

Another problem with developmental charts is that they can dilute the excitement that should accompany genuine milestones. If you're jumping for joy every time your baby passes some item from one hand to another or raises her head another 15 degrees, how are you going to react to the truly big moments like the first word or the first steps? Also, important turning points, like a baby gaining the ability to roll over (which can also be a safety issue, if, say, the child is lying on a changing table), can seem somewhat less significant when they're grouped into the same list of feats as "waving arms" and "screeching." (I have to admit, my daughter's first screech was a milestone reached without much rejoicing.)

It's also important to be aware that your child may tease you with "firsts" that don't stick. I heard from many a parent whose babies tried to make liars out of them, refusing to give a repeat performance

ARE YOU BEING PLAYED?

There's only one first time for everything, so whether it's because you're out for a run or just in the bathroom, you're going to miss some major milestones. For the working parent, chances are even greater that you (or your spouse) won't be around for some of them. This can be a big disappointment. One dad who happened to witness his son's first foray into walking felt so bad about the fact that his wife missed it that he decided to pretend it never happened, and then attempted a dramatic reenactment of those first steps when his wife came home. This was an admirable but risky gambit, as it required the cooperation of a baby to pull off.

If you're the parent who spends more time away from home, and you suspect you may be on the receiving end of such a benevolent con job, there are several clues to look for:

1. A suspicious number of baby's firsts happen to occur within five minutes of you stepping into the house.

2. You get phone calls at work that go like this:

   SHE: Are you still planning to stop on the way home and pick up diapers?
   YOU: Yep.
   SHE: Don't do it! Just come home.
   YOU: Oh, you got a chance to buy them today?
   SHE: Um . . . yeah.

   That night, you find your baby cruising around the coffee table—and no diapers in sight.

3. As your child takes his first solo stroll across the room, you notice your wife's misty eyes and loving smile are focused on you, not the kid.

4. Your wife and baby have a closed-door conference before allowing you into the room to suddenly hear the child gurgle, "Da-da!"

5. While still celebrating your daughter's just-witnessed ability to pull herself to her feet, the phone rings and your mother-in-law astounds you with her apparent precognitive abilities, responding to your "Hello" with, "So she's standing up by herself! That's so great. She'll be walking before you know it."

of a milestone that had already been announced to friends and family. Bryn did it to us with her first word. At around nine months, she shocked my wife and I by looking up as we entered the room and clearly shouting, "Hi!" We immediately got to work, phoning and e-mailing everyone we knew with the news that "Bryn said her first word! She said 'Hi!' Can you believe it?! 'Hi!'" We then went through several months of people glaring suspiciously at us as we hovered over our daughter going, "Say 'hi,' Bryn. C'mon, sweetie. Don't you want to say it? Say 'hi.'" It ended up being almost a year before she ever uttered that greeting again, though many other words came in between.

As much as I would like to tell you to Just Say No to charts altogether, doing so would be futile: Curiosity will get the better of you and you're going to look at them. And there's no way to avoid them completely, since a doctor will force them on you at regular well-baby visits. It's part of a pediatrician's job to tell you that your child is late on milestones A, B, C, and D, but not to worry about that, because being late is normal. If something's seriously wrong with your baby, the doctor will let you know. Beyond that, counting on developmental charts to tell you what your kid will be doing at any given point is as much of a sure thing as betting on the weather.

PART III

PEOPLE ARE STRANGE
(WHEN YOU'RE A FATHER)

To thrive in a foreign culture, one must familiarize himself with the ways and whims of its people. In Spain, you will learn that in order to leave a restaurant, you need to specifically ask for the check, because waiting silently for the wait staff to deliver your bill will result in you sitting around long enough to practically fall asleep counting the hams hanging from the ceiling. In Japan, you will come to realize buying squid out of a vending machine is considered totally normal. In fatherhood, you will discover that politely asking a stranger's six-year-old to stop shoveling sand onto your toddler's head at the playground may result in a vitriolic attack from the older boy's mother, where she accuses you of demeaning her parenting skills and calls you a name neither of the children should have heard.

What makes things all the more bizarre in the culture of fatherhood is that, unlike in international travel, much of the odd, unfamiliar behavior will come from people you already know. Of course, having a child also brings a surge of newcomers into your life—and there's quite a learning curve in establishing meaningful contact with those folks.

CHAPTER 5

You're Always a Child to Them

Whether you come from a bizarrely happy family where relatives joyfully sing together around the piano at regular gatherings or a classically dysfunctional one where people are threatened or guilted into singing together around the piano at gatherings, it will be impossible for your relationships with the kinfolk to remain the same now that you have become both parent and child. The birth of your baby will set off a seismic power shift, the ripple effects of which will upend the status quo between you and anyone who might be present to reach for that final drumstick at Thanksgiving dinner. But, of course, it's your own mom and dad (and your wife's) who are likely to be at the epicenter of the change.

THE SPOILERS: Grandparents Determined to Do Things *Their* Way

> "Fatherhood helped me understand the intensity of the parent-child relationship. It helped me let my parents off the hook for a lot of things." —Sachin W., Chicago, IL

Many grandparents see the birth of their grandchildren as a chance to reexperience all the fun parts of parenting with none of the responsibility: Thrill with no consequence—it's the same mentality that drives Civil War reenactors. This is why, as soon as possible, you must set ground rules with grandparents, perhaps even doing so in writing, to make sure they are 100 percent aware of your wishes when it comes to their interactions with your child. And then you must devise a backup plan for when those rules are inevitably ignored.

Just to be clear, your folks can be incredibly helpful. In many families, it is the grandparents who will be the most generous, the most willing to offer child-care assistance, and the quickest with words of encouragement. Still, even the best of them occasionally appear to take a devious pleasure in thwarting your most well-intentioned parenting plans. Sometimes when you drop your child off with your mother for an evening and ask her to hold off on sugary treats, you might hear her say "Yes," but see a twinkle in her eye that tells you that the minute you leave she's going: "No sweets, huh? Well, this is Grandma's house! *Mwa-ha-ha-ha-ha!* Open up, baby, here comes an Oreo!"

Perhaps it's payback for whatever difficulties you gave your folks when you were a kid (some grandparents have openly stated as much), but usually, we're not looking at malicious intent here. They *have* done this whole taking-care-of-a-baby thing before, and they're very secure in their belief that caring for your child will hold no surprises for them whatsoever. That's why as you're explaining, "The bottle lulls him right to sleep, so make sure he doesn't get one until just before bedtime or he'll go down too early and we'll be awake with him at two in the morning," your mother is just smiling, nodding, patting you on the back, and rushing you out the front door.

The possibility always exists that you will return from your outing to find your child snoozing hours before her regular bedtime with telltale chocolate cookie crumbs suspended in the drool at the corners of her mouth. And if your mother is confronted about her obvious transgressions, odds are she'll respond with a dismissive wave of her hand and, "*Eh,* she'll be fine."

One of the most common bits of advice today's grandparents have for the current generation of dads and moms is: "You worry too much." And they're right, we do. But every now and again, it's with good reason. Which is why it's so frustrating to hear your parents treat a warning like, "Children his age need to avoid peanut butter to lower the risk of a really nasty allergy," as if you just said, "We need to bathe him in goat's milk under the light of the full moon so the evil fairies won't swap him for a changeling."

Tolerating such mild annoyances is a small price to pay if it means your child will have loving, doting grandparents to add to her pantheon of "Big People Who Are Nice to Me." And perhaps you'll have an easier time accepting your parents' sigh-inducing behavior if we take the time to examine its origins—which often have their genesis in the following six words:

IT WAS GOOD ENOUGH FOR YOU

"The goal of life is to make fewer mistakes than your parents— or at least different ones."   —Andrew B., Milwaukee, WI

By now, you probably have a firsthand understanding of how easy it is to become paranoid that you're making all the wrong choices for your child. This particular breed of self-doubt seems to be able to linger for several decades, and sometimes your own folks are still going through it. Conflicts often arise when your parents or in-laws compare the way you choose to raise your kids today with the way they did things seven or eight presidential elections ago. How else could they interpret the fact that you use Huggies—rather than the Pampers your parents used to put on you—as, "You raised me like an animal, and I hate you for it!"

Grandparents who fall prey to this type of thinking tend to overlook the actual passage of time and forward march of progress, making them sometimes sound like the crazy old coots that fill Jerry Stiller's filmography ("Not even in school yet and she knows what an iPod is? You were happy with cassettes," "I don't understand all these soy products today. Who ever died from milk?" "You slept on this mattress for eighteen years, and now, suddenly, it's not safe?"). You do need to remember that back when our parents were giving us sharp metal toys to play with and dressing us in flammable pajamas, they weren't knowingly doing anything wrong. Horrifically dangerous children's products were the norm back then (today a dollhouse will be recalled if one superhumanly strong child manages to use a pair of vice grips to tear off the door and expose the hazardous screws inside). But even if you let your parents off the hook for not keeping up with every technological, medical, and dietary advance, there are some times when you feel you have to step in.

James K., a dad from Lafayette, Indiana, felt the need to speak up once while doing sixty-five down the interstate. "My mom was in the front, Dad in the back with my sleeping son," he explains. "My father hadn't been around young babies for a good many years, and this is the first grandchild in the family. I think he was a bit smitten and was playing a little with him back there. So naturally, the baby woke up and started crying. My dad said, 'Should I take him out of the car seat and hold him to calm him down?' I saw him reaching for the straps on the car seat. So while I'm trying to drive, I'm yelling, 'Dad! No! He stays in the car seat while the vehicle is in motion—even if he's crying!'"

Another Midwestern dad, put on guard by numerous articles about the dangers of *E. coli,* decided his baby daughter was not going to have any red meat—a stance he spelled out to his parents multiple times. "So my folks were watching the baby, and when we come to pick her up, I actually see my mother scraping clean plates from a hamburger dinner," he said. "They didn't even try to deny that they'd fed my daughter the specific thing I asked them not to. My father's defense was that, well, it was ground beef, it's not a choking hazard. I said, 'That's not the point!'"

These cross-generational misunderstandings are bound to give you at least a few "What the hell are they thinking?" moments with your parents. You need to be careful, though, that you don't automatically write off advice that might prove useful. After complaining about Bryn's teething-induced shrieking fits, both my mother and my mother-in-law advised using a little brandy to cure those ills. My wife and I were aghast at the idea of popping open the wet bar for our baby. With giddy disbelief ("My God, these women used to booze us up when we cried too much? How did we even survive to adulthood?") we filed the suggestion away in our anecdote drawer. Until one night at 3 a.m., after weeks of sleeplessness, I said "Screw it," staggered into the kitchen, dipped my finger into a bottle of Baileys, and rubbed it along my daughter's aching gums. Then the next morning, we were fully rested enough to call our moms and apologize.

If you find yourself beset upon by a deluge of unsolicited grandparent advice, the reason might also be that your parents assume you're always seeking advice—every time you speak to them. After all, why else would a grown man speak to his own mother or father if not to pluck some useful tidbits from their pupu platter of parenting wisdom? You especially need to watch out for this if you're the type of guy who has spent most of his adulthood without being super-close to his folks, and then ends up speaking to them a lot more often after the baby is born. Whenever one Southwestern dad needed to vent about the difficulties of adjusting to fatherhood, he'd call his mother—who would promptly tell him exactly how to solve all his problems. "It started bothering me," he told me, "and I finally had to tell her, 'Look, I'm not asking for constructive criticism; that's not why I'm telling you these things. Sometimes I just want to talk.' She understood, and now I think we're closer than ever. I talk to her probably four times a week."

LYING MEANS NEVER HAVING TO SAY YOU'RE SORRY: The Ups and Downs of Fibbing to Your Family

The easiest way to please your parents? Let them think you're doing everything just the way they would. Let's say you decided long before the birth that you were taking the disposable diaper route, but your father regularly comes around stumping for cloth, showing some kind of deep personal investment in it, and making you wonder if he's a silent partner in a diaper-cleaning service somewhere. It's nothing that a little head nodding won't fix.

Your parents don't want to have their wisdom written off, so the key is making sure they believe you're going to give their suggestions a shot. Memorize these Grandparent Appeasement Lines:

1. "Now, that's an idea."
2. "Wow, I never would have thought of that."
3. "We should give that a try sometime."
4. "Hmmm. Yeah. *Yeahhhhh.*"
5. "That's exactly what we were thinking of doing!"

Later on, if your parents follow up on how successful their suggestion was, tell them the baby was allergic.

You may also be tempted to skirt reality in regard to the gifts your child receives from grandparents. The easiest bad present to lie about is a piece of hideous clothing—think bauble-covered tracksuits more apropos of a casino buffet than a preschool, or frilly, giant-bow-bedecked garments that would look better on a Victorian doll. "We got one outfit that was so amazingly over-the-top; it was just completely covered with fabric roses, little fake pearls, and netting," said one dad. "We put it on our daughter for a Halloween party and had her go as a wedding cake."

In these cases, it's easy enough to tell your folks the outfits are very nice and then stow them in an under-the-bed box, only forcing your child to wear them when Grandma and Grandpa come over for a visit.

Sometimes your parents will make it all the more difficult to be truthful, not just with their bizarre choice of gift, but with their anxious longing to hear how much their grandchild liked the present. Take, for instance, when your mother asks about the baby's reaction to the four-foot-tall, red-eyed, cackling elf doll she sent him. The anticipatory joy in her voice lets you know she would crumble if she heard that her grandchild screamed in terror upon opening the box and hid in the recycling bin until the offending automaton was removed from the house.

Be careful if you choose obfuscation, since grandparents can interpret any gift "success" as a call for more of the same. If you decide to spare your mother by telling her that your son liked her gift—even with something as vague as "Yeah, I think he thought it was cute"—

she can take it to mean that she has struck gold. In her mind, your boy adores elves above all else, and your house will start filling with creepy little pointy-hatted manikins. It will all lead to one birthday when your mother is there in person to see your son open his present and witnesses his trembling sobs upon first glimpse of a green curly-toed foot under the wrapping paper.

Honesty is the only surefire way to avoid such a situation—and might even bring about the happy result of your parents starting to purchase gifts that don't make you cringe. If you do choose to tell the truth, be sure to do so after the *very first* inappropriate present, because if you don't rip that Band-Aid off quickly and your parents find out later on that you've been letting them waste their money, your relationship with them can suddenly get uglier than the stuff they've been buying for your kid.

NOT-SO-GRANDPARENTS

Many a man who reaches adulthood cradling a Fabergé-egg-fragile relationship with Mom and Pop hopes it will be repaired by their transition into grandparenthood. Sometimes it happens: The absentee father or self-involved mother recognizes this chance at a fresh start and morphs into an ideal grandparent. If things turn the other way, though, and your parents fulfill your *lowest* expectations, it can make a preexisting rift even wider, perhaps impassable.

While you might get ticked off by grandparents who hover a bit too much, genuine feelings are at stake when the grandparents show too little interest. I heard too many dads complain of apathy from their own mothers and fathers. "I keep trying to get my parents to interact with my son for his sake—I want him to have grandparents," said one East Coast dad. "I drop more hints than you could imagine:

'Well, he's going to be home all day on Saturday and we have no plans, so . . .' Never any response. It drives me crazy."

Some of the guys who harbored the most resentment felt their child was being used: The way they told it, their parents could never be bothered to go out of their way for the kids, but still wanted full grandparent privileges when the kids were brought to them.

"Because of my mother's general lack of involvement in our son's life, those rare occasions when we do see her are made even worse than they would have been otherwise," one D.C.-area dad explains. "She goes into overdrive and becomes Grandma-for-an-Hour. She'll be so in-your-face with the kid—hugging and kissing and smiling and pinching—and I get a little worried sometimes it's going to freak my son out, because, really, he barely knows this woman. It's like she's trying to cram an entire grandparent-grandchild relationship into the time it takes to watch a major motion picture. But, of course, she'll take tons of photos to show off to her friends."

Sadly, in the case of some grandparents, their own narcissism makes it difficult for them to bond with their grandchildren. "My mother simply does not go out of her way at all to have a relationship with my kids," said one dad. "I think it's less about me becoming a parent than it is about her becoming a grandparent. She says she's too young to be a grandmother, so it's difficult for her. With the magnitude of the transition *I'm* going through, I have no sympathy for her."

The members of this dysfunctional group certainly don't represent the whole of grandparentdom, but it's not impossible to find yourself stuck with one of them. Should that happen, it's important to remind yourself that you're the one with the child, and in the end it will be up to you to dictate how much of a relationship your parents get to have with that child. I spoke to one dad who made the difficult choice to cut off his mother entirely and has come to terms with that decision. "I got so tired of hearing her say, oh, she'd love to see my son, but then refusing to ever come to us to do that," he said. "She was willing to be a grandmother only when it was convenient for her, so I decided she didn't get to be a grandparent. My in-laws are great; they're all the grandparents my child needs."

LONG-DISTANCE GRANDPARENTING

In some families where the grandparents don't get to visit very often, it is not lack of interest that's the culprit, but geography. Growing up in the era that we did, more of us had grandparents and other extended family living nearby. Maintaining a relationship with relatives beyond our immediate families didn't require cross-country drives or thousands of dollars in plane fare. Today, with families often spreading out across multiple states, we may have to work harder to keep our kids connected with our own parents.

Figure in divorces, and your child can easily have grandparents in four different time zones. Voilà: logistical nightmare. Suddenly, in addition to being a new parent, you're also a travel agent. "You've got to manage the moms," one Southwestern dad told me. "I got a call from my mother on the East Coast: She wanted to see the baby for her birthday. I had to say, sorry, we're booked on the West Coast then. But we can fit you in for another holiday."

With any luck, you can get them to come to you, but even then, juggling visits is no simple task. "My parents and my wife's parents are both divorced, so Christmas feels like it lasts about a month for me," said another dad. "It's just one grandparent visit after another, all carefully coordinated so none of them cross paths."

Of course, your ability to fill out a calendar is not the only skill that will be tested with interstate grandparents. You will also face the rather daunting task of making sure your child can remember and keep track of grandparents she doesn't see in person very often. Phone calls are great, especially when the kid's a little older, but you might want to support them with pictures and other visual cues to which your child can connect the names ("That was Grandma Kate on the phone; she's the one in this photo with the curly hair; she sent you the finger paints. Got all that? Curly hair, finger paints, Grandma Kate"). If toddlers can learn who Winnie-the-Pooh, SpongeBob SquarePants, and Tony the Tiger are from nothing more than familiarity with their images, why not their grandparents? If you're lucky, your efforts will result in your child having the same reaction upon seeing your folks that she would upon seeing an underpaid college student in a full-body Pooh costume—the thrill of recognition. For a time, my mother-in-law was known as Grandma Glasses, but I think she was okay with that. It was better than Grandma Who?

On the grandparent end, current technology makes it a whole lot easier to see their grandkids grow up, even if they're hundreds of miles apart. Thanks to the Internet, digital video, and photo-sharing Web sites, family should be only a click away. Unfortunately, too many of today's senior citizens are still Luddites, leading to conversations like this:

YOUR FATHER: When are you going to take some pictures of that kid so we can remember what he looks like?

YOU: We have hundreds of pictures of him on Snapfish, Dad. I've told you that.

YOUR FATHER: Well, when are you going to send them to us?

YOU: I don't have to send them to you, Dad. They're on the Web site. Just go to Snapfish.com.

YOUR FATHER: (sighs) So how do I do this? Is it part of AOL?

YOU: No, Dad, just type in the URL. It's a Web site.

(silence)

YOUR FATHER: Can't you just send us some prints?

So, you can also add tech support to your new list of duties.

Before we leave the topic, I want to point out that there is a potential benefit to having your relatives scattered all about the nation: You'll have an all-purpose excuse for skipping out on family gatherings.

YOU CAN'T GO HOME AGAIN: A Family-Gathering Survival Guide

Happy holidays! Your present this year? Intense scrutiny and more than a few scares as your infant gets passed around like a tray of mini-quiches at a cocktail hour.

It may be only a matter of seconds after your arrival that the baby is swept away from you by an overly eager sibling. Then you can do no more than grit your teeth as you watch your tiny infant pass through a gauntlet of unfamiliar hands and slobbery kisses. A potential panic moment may occur when your child ends up in the arms of butterfingers Uncle Max who famously ruined Thanksgiving last year by losing his grip on the turkey as he attempted to deliver it to the dinner table. If you were to give in to your instincts, though, and shout, "Please, be careful! Her skull is still soft!" the entire clan would stop cooing at the child and start clucking at you: You will be instantly and forever branded a nervous, overprotective father.

Before we go any further: If your family gatherings are the kind of strife-free events marked by overly complimentary comments about casseroles and standing ovations for straight-A report cards—and if you participate in all these activities earnestly—then you might want to save yourself some time and just skip ahead to the next chapter. But if you're from a family where maybe everybody didn't vote the same way in the last election, or where at least a few exasperated sighs are heard at every call for a family photo, then you're familiar with the concept of get-together tension. This section is for you.

Family members can be just as judgmental about your choices as anybody else, perhaps even more so. Whether rightly or wrongly, relatives assume that, by dint of a shared bloodline, they have some stake in your child's upbringing. That presumption is a good part of what goes into making family gatherings so uncomfortable for new parents.

While you can tell a stranger on the street to screw off if he suggests you're not taking proper care of your child, you might not want to be so blunt with your relatives. You might not feel comfortable asserting yourself because you're among people who, on some level, still think of you as the little kid who wet his bed on Christmas Eve because he was afraid the Grinch would eat him if he ventured out to the bathroom. But even if your extended family has fully accepted your adulthood, you might choose to refrain from standing up against a pushy uncle because you fear it will open the door to black-sheep status.

At a family gathering, not accepting someone's unsolicited advice is akin to insulting them. So if you don't want to be the sower of discord, when your aunt hits you with some patronizing remark

("I'm sure you wouldn't realize this, but that baby should really have thicker socks on"), remember the Grandparent Appeasement Lines I mentioned earlier; they work with other relatives as well. Then go bitch about your aunt to someone who you know will happily commiserate.

"I considered our latest big family visit a success mainly because I decided to institute a policy of 'smile and nod' just to keep the peace," said one East Coast father. "I just vented to my brother when it was all over. It helped us both pull through."

Another easy way to offend someone at a family gathering is by displaying any doubt about that person's child-care abilities. It doesn't matter who they are—if they're related to you, *they can be trusted with the baby.* This means you cannot voice any concerns about the fifteen-year-old cousin who just offered to take the baby off your hands for a while—even though you know she managed to lose the family dog just a week earlier. Even if the teen herself would likely respond with a "Whatever," her mother would be appalled by your lack of confidence in her offspring—perhaps even to the extent of taking you off her greeting card list.

Instead of dismissing your cousin, tell her, "Thanks, but I'm really getting a kick out of showing off the baby to everybody myself." Or you can turn her down by deflecting your fears onto someone else: "Actually, I was just about to take the baby over to see Grandma, and I want to stick right nearby because Grandma's not exactly the steadiest ship in the sea, if you know what I mean."

If you're at a feast hosted on in-law territory, you may need to tread even more lightly and rely on your wife to deflect her more enraging relatives. Beyond that, just hope the people pushing you closest to the brink of "Don't make me angry; you wouldn't like me when I'm angry" are the relatives who flew in from out of state.

It can be hard to stay silent when your self-righteous brother-in-law implies that you should be jailed for letting your kid eat refined sugars. But remember, you're not giving him soapbox time because he's right; you're letting him speak because squeezing a bottle of French's into his face at a family picnic would cause your mother-in-law to forever refer to the day of the incident as "that one horrible Fourth of July."

And whenever the pressure gets too high, remember the baby: That bundle in your arms is your ticket out of almost any uncomfortable get-together. "We're able to leave gatherings early, using the child as an excuse," one dad admitted. "It's pretty sneaky, but whether or not people see through it, it always works because no one wants to be responsible for making a baby cry."

CHAPTER 6

Friends—The Good, the Bad, and the Ugly

Prior to becoming a parent, your friends may have fallen into a clearly defined pecking order, from your "call me any time of the night" confidant to the guy you've known since second grade but with whom you've never discussed anything deeper than a preference for specific episodes of *The X-Files.* After a baby enters your life, though, there will be an almost inevitable reshuffling. Some of your closest friends may begin to distance themselves. Others you rarely spent time with may prove far more understanding and considerate than you ever would have thought.

Even with friends who are already parents themselves, the jury will be out until you see how well your child-rearing style meshes with theirs. It is possible for twenty years of fond memories to get flushed down the drain when one guy holds a strong stance against corporal punishment and the other owns a wooden board inscribed with "Daddy's L'il Helper." But you don't need to rely solely on your old friends; you will also befriend other new parents—the surprisingly simpatico ones brought into your life by a combination of fate and a common playground, and those who you may not like very much but tolerate out of a need for emergency babysitting.

TRIAL BY DIAPER: Old Friends Put to the Test

At least a few close pals are likely to be excited about the idea of you having a baby. Most of your female friends will easily fit into this category, as will the guy friends who have at some point been labeled "great with kids" by your female friends—the ones who've played peekaboo with children waiting on line at the movies or turned down concert tickets because they were babysitting for their nieces. You will have no worries about these people.

You may also find that someone you'd previously considered a third-tier acquaintance pleasantly surpasses your expectations. Take the woman at work with whom you spend coffee breaks joking about your supervisor's midlife crisis earring. You may have never imagined that this friendship would reach beyond the walls of the office, but after she surprises you with a copy of *The Velveteen Rabbit* and an offer of her babysitting services, she may suddenly vault into a much higher echelon of friendship. It can be amazing how much someone's interest in your child comes to count in your estimation of them not only as a friend, but as a human being—which brings us to a sobering fact.

The man who has a child and still manages to retain all of his preexisting friendships should have traveling bards penning epic poems about him, for he is truly a man worthy of legend. A far greater likelihood exists that you'll have at least a few buddies who will start to see you differently—and whom you'll start to see a lot less of—once you're walking around with an infant strapped to your chest. Many of these not-so-positive reactions can be attributed to the fact that a lot of people (male *and* female) who don't have kids of their own honestly don't understand what it means to be a parent, neither the fatigue level and schedule constraints nor your honest desire to spend time with your baby.

The trick is figuring out which people truly care about you—or at least enjoy your company enough to accept new limitations on their time with you—and which ones have been friends with you solely because of your availability. Let's say a particular buddy's phone calls start becoming less and less frequent: His apparent willingness to let you fade from his life can make it that much easier for you to return the favor. Don't act too hastily, though. "Some friends assume my life is too hectic to include them, so they don't call," said Bradley C. from San Francisco. "When I ask them why we haven't spoken in so long, they say, 'We just thought you'd be too busy.' If you're available, and you're looking to see friends, call people and tell them."

You might also want to make sure that your friends' reluctance to call isn't stemming from the fact that you're one of those people who spend the majority of a phone conversation talking to his kid rather than the person on the other end of the line.

YOU: Hello.

CALLER: Hey, it's me. How's it going?

YOU: Oh, hey. Fine. I'm just hanging out with Duncan.

CALLER: How's the kid doing?

YOU: He's great. Aren't you, Duncan? Now don't put that in your mouth. You know better than that. Here, why don't you play with your drum, you like your drum. That's right. Good. Good.

CALLER: So . . . uh, seen any good movies lately?

YOU: What? Movies? Oh, no, not lately, but . . . Duncan, honey, what are you doing with those drumsticks? You're being so silly.

You should see what he's got on his head. Duncan, take that off, you big goof. (pause) What are you doing?

CALLER: Well, I just got a promotion, which I'm kind of excited about.

YOU: Oh, no, sorry, I was talking to Duncan. Duncan, what are you doing?

But, of course, some of your friends may just be clueless, and their behavior around your child may perplex you ("I'll just never understand why my guy friends can't walk down the street with me without bumping into the stroller," said one dad) or frustrate you ("I don't mind my friends drinking beer around my two-year-old," said another, "but why can't I get them to understand that they can't put an open bottle down within the baby's reach?"). What really matters, though, is whether they're making an effort. Even if someone is generally awkward around kids, you can appreciate the fact that he's sticking around. It could possibly endear him to you more, since you know he's stepping out of his comfort zone to spend time with you. Just be sure to respect the guy's boundaries and don't invite him out for an afternoon at Chuck E. Cheese's.

Occasionally, a friend may grow resentful of your new family when his share of your attention gets downsized. If you thought the clueless ones were annoying, a jealous or disdainful friend prone to sarcasm can make the inventor of Caller ID your new hero. It's easy to grow tired of a friend who rolls his eyes at any mention of your baby, mocks the new strained-pea-spattered aesthetic of your home, and hits you with questions like "What, you can't pick up the phone anymore?"

"I've had it up to here with the 'What ever happened to you, man?' e-mails," said one New York dad.

Some friends make things worse by looking upon your parenthood as some form of betrayal against the indie culture they imagine themselves to belong to ("Dude, you totally sold out"). As a family man, you're now part of the Establishment: These friends will view you having a baby the same way they would you buying a Kelly Clarkson CD.

Still, if the friendship has a strong enough foundation, you can keep it together. A lot of dads are able to give their childless friends some leeway, since they, themselves, can remember having a similar lack of empathy in the past. "Whenever I used to visit friends of mine who were parents, I'd think, oh man, I hope we don't spend the whole time looking at his kid—babies are boring," admits Chris F. of Las Vegas. "Now that I've got a child of my own, I don't want to be the guy who makes his friends come over and stare at his kid—even though, ironically, I would now be very happy to spend an evening doing just that. My daughter is so cute."

That said, realize that some old friends, namely the antichild people, are lost causes. Maybe you used to tolerate your old college roommate's bloviations about zero population growth because you always thought he was half-joking or because he entertained you with impressions of Cartman from *South Park* more often than he inveighed against "breeders." But once you have come to know the intensity of love fathers can have for their children, it's hard to sit through anyone's rant about how disgusting the little beasts are without wanting to empty your Diaper Genie onto his head. What's worse, though, is when your friend hides his antichild leanings and feigns tolerance of your kid's presence. Before long, the time will come when you innocently ask the guy to hold the baby for a moment while you run to the john, only to be stunned by his exclamation of "Sorry, dude, I just can't handle this." Life, and parenthood in particular, is too short to waste time with people who can't control their fear of baby cooties.

One former acquaintance of mine—the type of guy who was too cool for his own good (think leather in August)—was prone to overly theatrical shudders whenever a family with children entered the restaurant where we were dining. I'd roll my eyes, but say nothing, because I believed he was a generally decent guy and an entertaining conversationalist. Upon his first introduction to my daughter, the only words he was able to eke out were, "You have a baby." He kept muttering that phrase over and over, in a manner reminiscent of Brando's "The horror, the horror" from *Apocalypse Now*. That was the last time I saw him, and I can't say I'm too upset about it.

SOCIALIZING WITH NON-PARENTS: A PRIMER

- **When You're Out Without The Baby . . .** Keep baby-related talk to a minimum. Friends worth keeping will ask about your child, because they care enough not to ignore this very important part of your life. But that still doesn't mean they'll want to hear the minute, graphic details of your baby's day ("So I can't help but wonder, if he's not even eating solid foods yet, why do his bowel movements look like they're full of mustard seeds?"). "You have to know the exact amount of time you can spend talking about the kid," said New York dad Nick Tucker. "If it's all about the kid, your friends can't relate. You have to know your audience."

  It also helps to feign a lack of worry about the state of things back home. It may be disheartening for your non-parent friend to hear, "Sorry, I missed what you said. I just remembered that I totally forgot to tell my wife where I put the duck-headed hoody towel."

- **When You're Out With The Baby . . .** Remember to look at the adults. Friends understand that you need to pay attention to the child, but they can get justifiably irked if you seem preoccupied through an entire meal.

"We were eating at T.G.I. Friday's with a friend of ours, and I was talking to him while I was spoon-feeding my son," one dad told me. "At first, I got really annoyed when my friend said, 'Hello, I'm over here.' But then I realized I'd responded to a question he asked me with something totally unrelated. I really wasn't listening to him."

Also, if both parents are there, always put the baby between the two of you. Unless another dinner companion specifically requests to sit next to the kid, assume he doesn't want to. A good friend is not going to ask you if he can sit farther away from your child, so don't trap him into sitting right next to the high chair unless you're hoping to get a good laugh from seeing him jump away from your baby's ketchup-coated fingers like a cartoon elephant who has just seen a mouse.

- **When Friends Come to Your Place . . .** There should be at least a cursory attempt to make your house look like adults live there. This includes clearing a walking path from room to room: You may have developed a trained rat's ability to navigate the maze of swings, play tables, and safety gates, but your guests have not. Also, make sure there are dry places to sit.

And unless your friends have stopped by explicitly to see the baby, it's nice to have some way of allowing the child to occupy himself for at least part of the visit. An Exersaucer, a video of toy trains, or a nap can go a long way toward preventing your friends from feeling like a trip to your house is really four hours of group babysitting in disguise.

THE OLD PROS: Friends with Kids

If you're lucky enough to be close with people who already have children, you've got a built-in reference desk, built-in babysitting, and built-in counseling from people who understand your concerns because they've been where you are. So first off, get back in their good graces by apologizing for being such a jerk the whole time you were their childless friend. Then milk them for everything they've got.

However, having a child of your own is not always the surefire hit you might expect it to be with other parents. It all depends on how well your child-rearing styles mesh. A philosophy clash can kill a friendship, even between couples who have been close for ages. If there's one thing you must always keep in mind when relating to other people with children, it is that parents can be unbelievably petty.

What it all comes down to is the fact that a lot of people are terrified of being bad parents (or at least of being perceived as bad parents). They invest a lot of emotional energy into the belief that their choices are the right ones. Allowing that anybody else's vastly different style might also work puts their own in question (you can't have *two* best ways!). So, no quarter is given.

Now, you'd think that people who have been friends for years would cut each other a little slack, and sometimes they do. But, as I mentioned earlier in this book, there are folks who like to wear their parenting philosophy on their sleeve. If you don't happen to share in their zealotry, trying to maintain an amicable relationship with them can be as difficult as a logger spending a nice, restful afternoon at an Earth First! rally.

Say you've opted to sleep-train your baby in her own bassinet. Whether the process is working well or not, you don't want to hear your friend tout the virtues of the "family bed" in every conversation you have with him. It won't take long for the constant proselytizing to feel like a harsh judgment on your own chosen sleeping arrangements. This can happen even if your friend insists it's not his intent ("Oh, please don't take it that way—just because *we* feel it would be inhumane to sleep-train *our* child doesn't mean it's not a valid choice for yours").

Mega-issues like sleep and discipline are obvious sources of friction. But there can be a billion little variations in the ways two couples choose to parent—and each one harbors a potential pet peeve. If your friends feel totally secure with their newly mobile baby scuttling his way up and down the stairs, they're not going to zip out and buy a pressure-lock safety gate just because you flinch every time your toddler teeters near the top of their steps. Or let's say you purposely refrain from using profanity in front of your child; knowledge of that fact may not stop your friends from going HBO around the kids if that's their home standard. You can let these transgressions slide, explaining to your child that different kids live by different rules (and praying she'll understand that lesson), or allow the contentious issues to become parasitic worms that slowly nibble away at a friendship until there's nothing left but the occasional nod to each other on the street.

Sometimes *you* might be the one unknowingly offending your friends. And one day, you will do something that you think of as innocuous, but they consider too egregious to overlook. That's what happened to my wife and me at our friends' daughter's third birthday party. When the little girl unwrapped the edutainment videotape we'd given her, her parents glared at us as if we'd just shat on their carpet. It was the first realization we had of how much they'd been judging us. They were apparently strict no-TV parents, and though they'd never criticized us for letting Bryn take in the occasional program, we must have crossed a line when we brought the contraband into their own home. There was no exchange of harsh words after that, no big blowup, just a subtle slowing down of communication. At this point, even the e-mails have petered out.

A. The Invasion of the Visiting Brat

No one *wants* to dislike their friends' children. But chances are, if enough people in your social circle begin to procreate, eventually one of them will give birth to some sniveling homunculus that will terrorize your home and torment your own kid. And you can't even tell in the first year or so, before the kid is physically able to cause much trouble, whether your friend has spawned the Bad Seed. Too many people I know have infants right now—I'm bracing myself.

Any desire you have to respect other people's parenting styles is admirable. However, it's understandably difficult to exhibit restraint when a friend—say, a staunch believer in the use of gentle reasoning to bring his toddler out of a tantrum—is all-too-calmly attempting to talk his son down from an unrelenting assault on your home-entertainment center ("Now, I understand that you're upset, honey. And that's okay. You're allowed to have feelings. But we know it's not good to pound our friend's DVD player with that dump truck. Don't you think we should stop, honey? Honey?"). And while you may feel that intervening in such a situation should be entirely acceptable, your friend could very well take it as a personal assault on his choices as a parent. So even if you don't intend it to, "Please take him away from there—my warranty expired last month," can come across as a vicious attack.

One Midwestern dad complained about being stuck in a similar situation with a buddy of his who would often come over for dinner with his three sons. The visiting boys would inevitably end up grabbing their fish sticks and running to eat them in every area of the house other than the dining room. He felt bad telling his own daughter she couldn't join her friends and had to eat at the table, because that was the regular house rule. "Plus," he added, "I'd always have to clean up the mess." Still, he struggled for a long time over how to confront his old pal without insulting him.

Worrying about a politically correct way to intercede becomes much less of an issue if safety comes into play. Your need to protect your own child will often trump your desire to be polite; for example, you'll be a lot less likely to worry about stepping on any proverbial toes if some sadistic kid is getting his jollies by stomping on your daughter's actual digits.

By the way, that Midwestern dad worried that a rift would grow between his friend and him if the toddler rampages continued, so he asked the guy to keep his sons at the table during dinner. It was an uncomfortable moment to be sure, but now that it's over, the two are still on good terms.

B. A Dad-Eat-Dad World: Unfriendly Competition

An ounce of pride about being a good parent is to be expected. But things can get out of hand if playful boasting devolves into an outright competition between you and your dad friends. Each time another father shows off some fancy new baby gadget he's acquired or proudly announces his kid's latest awe-inspiring developmental leap, you might feel like he's just taunted, "It's your move."

Even if you're not a hypercompetitive guy, you can still find yourself infected by the One-upmanship Virus. That's when your need to be a "good father" gets pushed past the brink of reason by another dad's grandiose self-promotion. You might start to hear Sean Connery's voice in your head, haranguing you with the fatherhood version of his *Untouchables* speech: "He buys an expensive Scandinavian stroller with shock absorbers—you buy an ergonomic titanium model with four cup-holders. He sends his kid to ballet class—you send yours to soccer camp, piano lessons, *and* circus arts."

This is not healthy. It can lead to a busted bank account and a child whose life is so overscheduled that he panics and wilts the first time he's told to occupy himself for a few minutes. It's great to give your child access to as many enriching activities and new experiences as possible, but it's also good to step back every now and again and see if you're doing these things for the kid's benefit, or out of a desire to feel better about yourself whenever you hear about another guy installing a ball pit in his rec room.

On the flip side of competition is feigned compliance—when a pal's sheepish admissions to less-than-stellar parenting behavior have you copping to things you don't do or condoning behavior you don't agree with. A lot of the guys I interviewed admitted that being judgmental is an unfortunate but unavoidable side effect of parenthood. But most agree that what separates a good friend from a bad one is the ability to keep those critical opinions unvoiced.

"Dads are more forgiving of one another, because we want more forgiveness ourselves," said Casey S. of Sacramento, California.

One time, while out with another dad, I watched him repeatedly refill his on-the-way-to-overweight two-year-old's gigantic sippy cup with Pepsi. As he topped his son off for the fourth time in an hour, the guy looked at me plaintively, and said, "He just never wants to drink anything else." Now, my daughter isn't exactly a paragon of dietary excellence—in fact, she and Annie's Mac & Cheese are probably sustaining each other—but we at least *try* to keep junk food to a minimum. I wanted to say, "He's two—*make* him drink something else!" Instead, to prevent our future get-togethers from being awkward, I said, "Well, you can't let him go thirsty, right?"

More often, I find myself going in the opposite direction, pretending to be more concerned about a certain issue than I actually am. Such was the case when a friend vented to me about all the strain she was under from trying to keep her child entertained for hours on end. When she asked me how I managed to deal with it, I didn't answer with, "I tell Bryn to play by herself for a while." Instead, I expressed sympathy: "It's tough; I just try to focus on the parts of playing with my kid that are fun for me, too." I wasn't lying; I just didn't mention that I don't think it's the end of the world if a kid has to entertain herself every now and again.

You don't like anybody else telling you how to raise your kid, so you endeavor not to do so yourself. You're just being considerate. Realistically, however, if there are deep ideological differences that you and a friend are both stifling, you're probably not in the most secure relationship to begin with. Plus, there's a fine line between supporting a friend's right to parent in his own way, and aiding and abetting.

You don't want an exchange like this:

FRIEND: "You don't think it's too bad that I let her watch *The Deer Hunter*, do you?"

YOU: "Come on, Christopher Walken wasn't half as scary then as he is now."

to end up in a place like this:

FRIEND: "If she refuses to get in her crib, do you ever let her sleep in the bathtub?"

YOU: "*Pffft!* Who doesn't?"

MARRIED FATHER SEEKS SAME FOR PLAYDATES, HAND-ME-DOWNS: Making New Parent-Friends

If you happen to be among the first of your social circle to have kids, finding new parent-friends will become your own personal quest for the Holy Grail. It's not that literally locating other parents is difficult—they're everywhere; hard to avoid, in fact. The challenge lies in determining which of the lot might make potential good friends.

You'll probably start your search in a place where you see the same parents regularly. If your child is in any kind of class—preschool, arts and crafts, baby tap—you're bound to have a cast of recurring characters to choose from. In such a setting, you're more likely to know the names of the kids than those of the moms and dads. This is because, during the twenty-five minutes it takes to bundle your toddler into her snowsuit before you can exit the building, you will hear all the other pickup parents constantly repeating their children's names ("Time to go, Imani," "What on earth is caked under your nails, Dmitri?"), while all the grown-ups are simply "Daddy" or "Mommy." With all these equally unknown parents milling about, you may be at a loss as to whom you should approach.

Then you will see your child cheerily greet one of the other adults ("Hi, Dylan's daddy!'). And this cipher of a person will respond to your kid by name. As weird as it may feel to witness such an exchange, recognize that your child has essentially just opened the door for you. I have started more than one conversation with, "Well, I see you've met my daughter. . . ."

If classes aren't your thing (or even if they are), there are scads of other places to meet parents, starting with that old stalwart, the playground. One thing that works in your favor when it comes to meeting other dads is the fact that most guys tend to arrive at the swing sets without an entourage. Mommies, on the other hand, often show up at the playground in cliques and spend hours engaged in lunch-table-style girl-talk while their preschoolers work out some adrenaline on the monkey bars. When it comes to a new woman gaining admission, these playground coteries might as well be the Augusta National Golf Club. As a man, you have a slight advantage in the friend-making department in that the other guy sitting by himself on the edge of the sandbox, watching his son sift for lost toys with a plastic colander, is probably far more amenable to casual conversation. Still, if you're not the type who takes easily to spontaneous chitchat with people you've never met before (perhaps the voice of McGruff the Crime Dog warning you not to talk to strangers at the playground has been ingrained in your psyche since childhood), you may find this difficult.

> "Most men don't really want to speak face-to-face with other men about parenting. I don't know if it's an ego or socialization thing, but we mostly figure we're supposed to muddle through alone somehow. Probably because that's what our fathers did."
> —James K., Lafayette, IN

Here's the problem: Guys don't talk to one another. Oh, we'll blather on about politics, business, pop culture, or sports until our lips go numb, but any conversation that might reveal some vulnerability is anathema to most men. I can count on one hand (one Simpson hand would do) the number of guys with whom I can discuss deeper issues. And that's not unusual.

"I have this fear of becoming an older man with no close friends other than my spouse," said Christopher P. of San Francisco. "The only way to stop that from happening is to meet people and really open up; have conversations rather than just hang out. If you're not actually sharing things with the other guy during the time you spend with him, what do either of you have invested in the friendship?"

With parenting being such a volatile issue, leaping into shoptalk with dads can be even more difficult than it is with other guys. Insecurity ("If I ask questions, will it look like I don't know what I'm doing? What if he does things completely opposite from me and his kid is some kind of miracle child?") and machismo ("I've got things under control; I don't need to hear some other guy yakking about how he raises his kid") can both be obstacles. But the potential benefits of having new parent-friends outweigh the risk of possibly being snubbed by a dad with too much self-doubt or stubborn bravado of his own.

"In the beginning, I never wanted to be pushy at the playground, but no other parents ever came over to me to start talking," said Jeffrey F. of New York City. "I knew I'd have to initiate those conversations if I wanted to have them, and the two things that drove me to do it were my own fear of loneliness and the fact that my son deserves playmates. If he was going to have any real friends, I was going to have to get to know their parents."

At the very least, choosing a topic to start the dialogue with should be a no-brainer. At the park or the kids' corner of your local bookstore or the waiting room of a pediatrician's office, there's always that little living icebreaker tugging at your pant leg. You've got a kid, he's got a kid—boom.

"I had a great conversation with another male English teacher at the high school where I did my student teaching. He and I never talked much in the days before then, but discovering our common kid situation created an instant connection between us. I can't imagine anything else we could have talked so openly about in such a short time." —Kevin K., Perth, Australia

---

BOY MEETS GIRL

Ridiculous as it may be, a solo dad hitting up a solo mom for small talk at the park can often be a dicey situation. "It's difficult talking casually to the moms," one dad admitted. "You know, there's all that heterosexual tension. It's too complicated to navigate."

It shouldn't have to be this way. You and this unaccompanied mother you might meet are both responsible adults; rather than the two of you silently zoning out to the grinding sounds of circling Big Wheels while your children each push their teddy bears on the baby swings for hours, you should be able to engage in a meaningful exchange of parenting information or perhaps some entertaining repartee about the bizarre psychedelia of British kids' shows. Instead, you must be concerned that: (a) she doesn't think you're a lecherous creep sidling up to hit on her; (b) other parents at the park don't think you're a lecherous creep sidling up to hit on her; and (c) you don't accidentally hit on her.

Blame the *When Harry Met Sally* paradigm, which holds that platonic male-female friendships are as realistic a prospect as widespread use of the Segway. Of course, this is just a myth perpetuated by a never-ending stream of "When will they finally do it?" sitcoms. But that doesn't mean that the woman you meet by the jungle gym (or your wife—or you) won't wonder if there's some truth to it. Potentially awkward moments always lie in wait, despite the fact that, in reality, a young father *can* casually befriend a young mother without having the relationship turn into fodder for some Lifetime network Jennie Garth vehicle—even if that mother is really hot.

BOB AND CAROL AND TED AND ALICE AND THEIR KIDS: Family Dating

As part of a couple with a child, you may have thought your dating days long over, but, alas, they are only just beginning. Once you have children, many of your friendships become much less about two people, or even two couples, than they are about two families.

For a new parent-friendship to have real long-term potential, you must embark upon a series of family dates. Unless you and your partner hooked up at a research station in Antarctica and haven't left since, you've probably experienced couple dating. You know the challenges involved: If, say, the woman in the other couple is very pleasant but her husband gives you involuntary spasms every time he snorts at one of his own awful one-liners, the whole four-person dynamic is thrown off. Family dating raises the difficulty by several degrees, since not only do all the adults have to get along, but they have to be able to tolerate each other's kids, and the kids need to like one another, too.

Still, family dating is the only way to find out if you really want to get to know these people. In many cases, you'll come to realize upon first gathering that this particular social mix is definitely not going to work (while emptying their picnic bags, one wife's Ann Coulter book lands upon the other woman's Howard Zinn). But even if all goes well, one smooth outing does not guarantee success. Sometimes even the first few impressions can be misleading. It can take a while before people start truly being themselves on their family dates.

Should things go well over time, you or they may want to take these dates beyond brunch at whatever local diner provides its customers with lidded cups. Finally hearing "So you guys want to come back to our place?" can set off the same kind of inner electric tingle you felt the first time your elementary school crush's best friend passed you a folded note that read "Susie thinks she might maybe like you."

Moving these dates into either family's home is a major step, because only when you see a couple on their own turf do you truly get a glimpse of their parenting style, unedited. The transformation you see may be jarring, but just keep your fingers crossed in the hopes that your two families still gel even after you've seen one another's reaction to the wall-mounted sculpture the kids constructed out of pilfered Fruit Roll-Ups while the grown-ups were talking. If one set of parents starts admiring the composition and color scheme of the sticky artwork ("I like the way they swirled the blueberry around the cherry in that double helix") while the other explodes like a couple of latter-day Sam Kinisons, you might not have a good match.

Whether it's through irreconcilable differences in parenting style or the discovery that you and the other person just really dislike each other, there are numerous ways in which to lose a new parent-friendship—which is why those that stick are relationships to be treasured. And because the children from both couples will probably continue to interact even after the parents' relationship ends, it's important to make those partings as amicable as possible (i.e., no cursing the eternal souls of people you may some day serve with on a PTA committee).

CHAPTER 7

Who Are the People in Your Neighborhood?

"Before my son was born, I imagined I'd be part of a global community of parents. Since then I've come to the realization that I just don't like most of them." —Tavis A., New York, NY

Oh, the parents you'll meet! Some will be so uptight that they panic any time their children get exposed to anything with a remote element of danger ("Would you mind if I took the kids away from the s-l-i-d-e; I'm afraid if my daughter sees it, she may want to try it"). Others will be so laissez-faire in their parenting that they think nothing of a three-year-old playing with a Zippo ("Don't worry, he won't figure out how to work it"). For the sane father, finding a safe path between paranoid anxiety and reckless disregard is no easy task. And yet we must find a way to peacefully coexist with parents who personify these extremes . . . for the sake of the children.

PLAYDATE POLITICS: Should I Stay or Should I Go?

Once upon a time, if Billy wanted to play with Timmy, Billy's parents could drop their boy off at Timmy's house and go home by themselves to clean out their attic, watch an R-rated movie, or engage in some other activity that is better done without a child present. But that was before the dawn of the playdate. Today when Timmy's folks say, "Why don't you bring Billy over for a playdate?" those words hold an unspoken invitation—really an *expectation*—for Billy's parents to stick around as well. A "playdate" is when two children meet at an arranged time and place to have some fun together, and the parents of those children, well, stay there.

One East Coast dad said he arranged a "playdate" for his daughter without being aware of the very specific connotations that term carried. "So Saturday comes and both the parents show up with their daughter. My wife invited them in, and because we didn't really know them at all, I figured they were going to just introduce themselves, kiss their daughter good-bye, and be off," he explains. "About fifteen minutes later, I'm thinking, Okay, they're giving their kid some time to adjust before they go; maybe their girl has big attachment issues or something. After a half hour, though, they're still sitting on our couch, and I start thinking, Oh my God, they're not leaving, are they? I mean, they were really nice people—I have absolutely nothing against them—but it was pretty clear from about the twenty-minute mark that there wasn't enough in common between the four of us to sustain multiple hours of conversation."

The difference between a playdate and a family date is that on the family date, you are hoping to become friends with the other child's parents. On a playdate, you may have no such designs; it's all about your kid getting to work out some energy with someone his own size. Now, you might be wondering, if this playdate is all for my child's sake, and I have no desire to get chummy with the other adults, shouldn't I be allowed to just leave my kid there to play and come back to pick him up later? Of course you should! That's simple logic.

But you can't. It's against the rules.

A lot of guys I spoke to are insulted by the formal playdate system, because they say it reflects the lack of trust between parents. If other parents were to leave their child in your hands, and return later on to discover that, in their absence, the kids were allowed to eat Pixie Stix, or jump on the bed, or listen to Toby Keith records, they would be racked with guilt—not to mention pissed at you for undermining their child-rearing plans without even being a grandparent.

So that explains why other parents refuse to leave. But if you have complete faith in the other couple, why can't you drop off your kid with them? Shouldn't they be flattered that you think highly enough of them to do so? Perhaps. But it's more likely they'll assume you're trying to scam free babysitting out of them (which, in reality, you are—not that there's anything wrong with that).

In an ironic twist, it really only becomes socially acceptable to let your child play unchaperoned at another couple's house after you have become close friends with that couple—at which point, you'd probably *want* to spend time with them, anyway.

Hyperparents love the mandatory attendance rule. It gives them just one more way to brag about how they have no time for anything except their kids. Having to spend hours at playdates is another welcome obligation for people who love to say things like, "Read the newspaper? What, do they still print those things? I don't know, I've got a kid." So, remember, while you and Billy's dad are sitting there watching your children assemble an eight-piece puzzle for the fifteenth time, you're not supposed to want or need to do anything else. Enjoy yourself.

THREE STEPS TO PLAYDATE SURVIVAL

1. **Make believe you're happy.** Remember, it's all for the kids, so get your game face on. Even if the other adult is boring the hell out of you, smile, damn it. "Playdates fail when the other parent is a downer," said Jeffrey F. of New York City. "You regret inviting them over when you realize too late that this playdate is just a chance for the other guy to get out of his house and vent."

   Don't let a bad conversation partner sink your child's good time: Commandeer the dialogue. And if need be, filibuster until it's time for everybody to go home.

2. **Muffle your beliefs.** I'm not saying you should compromise your own values just to make another parent happy on a playdate. But use a little discretion. If your playdate partner has his kid snacking on nothing but cucumber slices, telling your son, "Don't forget to share your pork rinds with your friend," is not polite; it's passive-aggressive.

3. **Count the awkward pauses.** It's a great way to pass the time. Think of it as something similar to those road-trip games where you try to spot a license plate from every state. Each time you have a playdate, keep track of how many uncomfortable silences occur between you and the other parent. Then, try to beat that record on your next playdate!

IT'S MY PARTY AND I'LL BUY IF I WANT TO

First of all, yes, you also have to stay for parties. What, are the other twelve parents there supposed to be in charge of your kid, too?

But being a guest at a child's birthday celebration is a cakewalk compared with hosting one. Nowhere does the competitive nature of modern parenthood show itself more than at parties. Events that don't need to consist of much more than ice cream and pin-the-tail-on-the-donkey are turning into red-carpet-worthy galas. Pony rides and moon bouncers used to be signs that the day's honoree was probably rich enough to have a butler unwrap his gifts for him. Now such attractions are as common among minivan owners as they are among the Bentley set.

The more today's parents worry about being outperformed by their neighbors, the more profitable the birthday party industry becomes. Today, birthday party expos hit cities all over the country, letting parents know just how inadequate a game of musical chairs would be when fire-truck visits or private zoo tours are real options. A May 2005 article in the *Arkansas Democrat-Gazette* quoted a mother at the Little Rock expo who said she'd coughed up more than two hundred dollars for her four-year-old's birthday, and would "be looking to spend that much" for her one-year-old, too. "She loves her kids and wants them to know it," the reporter added.

So there you have it: Love is now equated with the rental of inflatable castles.

Even if your child's party won't involve attractions delivered on flatbed trucks, you've still got your work cut out for you. Today's most modest parties are still major to-dos. First of all, you *must* have a theme. Usually based around a favorite fictional character, the birthday theme will manifest itself in decorations, cake design, organized games, piñatas, goodie-bag contents, and perhaps even costumes for the young guests. A fiesta with monochromatic balloons and plain chocolate cookies will be forgotten by the time the children walk out the door, but, as party supply Web site Birthday Direct.com says, "Thirty-five years later, kids will remember their Strawberry Shortcake party."

May I remind you that we're talking about preschoolers here.

One time my wife took our toddler out for a full day's worth of activities—a few errands, followed by a trip to the zoo, a carousel ride, and a magic show; when they came home and I asked Bryn to tell me about all the fun she had, her response was, "We went by the shoe store. It was closed."

The most pointless parties are those thrown for a baby's first birthday. Not that you shouldn't celebrate such an occasion—of course you'd want to—but I find it hard to see the necessity in confetti, streamers, and hourly rate clowns for an infant who still looks at a ride in a shopping cart as the adventure of a lifetime. We should all just admit that first birthday parties are strictly for the parents, since a one-year-old is as cognizant of the occasion as the average adult is of Arbor Day. If we acknowledge that, we can throw a nice grown-up party that everybody can enjoy—and just give some presents to the kid while we're there.

As the number of candles increases, you need to put in a little more effort, because it takes more to entertain the kids—but not much more. I think I could throw the ultimate kid's party on a budget of about $20: I'd invite four or five preschoolers over and give them all a big piece of cake immediately upon entering (what two-year-old wants to wait for dessert?). Then I'd put on an *Elmo's World* DVD. While the parents all chatted with one another over guacamole and chips in the dining room, the kids would run around the living room unsupervised until they burned off their sugar highs. On their way out, I'd hand each young guest the parting gift of an empty cardboard tube.

The adults would be aghast. But I bet the kids would love it.

HOSTILE ENCOUNTERS: What Is Wrong with These People?

No matter how much trouble you go through to avoid any ugliness between you and other parents, the fact is that, whether mildly aggravating or downright belligerent, there are enough assholes out there to make such a goal eternally unobtainable. It's pretty much inevitable that you'll run into open confrontation at some point in your parenthood. The only question is: How bad will it be? Consider the following true-life examples:

- **The Day-Care Drop-Off Duel.** You're on the way to drop your kid off at her child-care center. Some other dad coming from the opposite direction sees you pushing your stroller toward the entrance and decides to play chicken. Why is he in such a rush? What could possibly make him risk his own baby's safety just to beat you to the doorway? You'll never know. But before Peg-Péregos collide and tots are jostled, you hit the brakes to let Kenickie pass. It's the kind of out-of-the-blue antagonism that, without the exchange of any words, can sour you on another person for life. From that point on, your eyes will narrow upon the sight of that approaching speed demon and his baby-bearing juggernaut.

- **The Bookstore Brush-Off.** You're browsing the shelves for Maurice Sendak books while your son sits among a group of toddlers flipping through the pages of poorly written movie tie-ins. Suddenly, you hear a woman speaking to her daughter, in a stage whisper that lets you know her words are really meant for you: "No, sweetie, just let *that little boy* have the book. I know *you were reading it first,* but *he* wants to see it now. He probably *doesn't know any better,* but you can show him what a *good girl you are* and let *that little boy* keep the book."

You turn around, and, ignoring her obnoxious tactics, apologize: "I'm sorry, did he take your daughter's book?" You give your son a few quick words about not taking other people's things, and hand the book to the girl.

Not only are your attempts at reconciliation rebuffed, but the woman still refuses to speak to you directly, instead saying to her child: "Don't be upset, honey, just because that man *thinks you don't know how to share.* He just doesn't know what a good girl you are." And they storm off. What crime did you commit to receive such disdain? Is she trying to sculpt her daughter into some kind of mini-misanthrope? It's a mystery.

- **The Playground Provocation.** You're sitting on a bench watching your two-year-old daughter toddle up the steps to the top of the little slide in the "Ages 4 and Under" play area. Well-warranted concern sets in when a six-year-old comes zipping through, flailing a wooden sword. Why is the mother of the rampaging grade-schooler sitting under a tree with a paperback, rather than taking her son to a more age-appropriate part of the playground? Why is she letting her child play with a toy that could easily give any adult a concussion in the first place? These questions will go unanswered. But obviously this is a moment when you have to act. And I did, as I was the unfortunate protagonist of this last scenario. I tried to give the oblivious parent the chance to do the right thing, drawing her attention to the problem with a few throaty "ahems." When my phlegmy protests went unheard, I pondered the possibility of simply removing my daughter from harm's way, thereby

RULES TO PLAY BY

1. **If your kid's too big for it, keep him off it.** That means no ten-year-olds contorting themselves to fit into infant swings. If there are no big-kid swings available, the truant fourth-graders at the playground will just have to deal.

2. **If your kid's too small for it, keep him off it.** That means no newbie walkers straddling the rope bridge. The other parents have to watch their own kids; don't give them cause to start rubbernecking over yours.

3. **If your kid looks like he could hurt others, stop him.** It doesn't matter that you have total faith in your preschooler's ability to veer around other tots as he careers through the playground with the recklessness of the bus from *Speed*; other parents are not aware of his lightning reflexes and preternatural agility. They will be frightened. Rein your child in for their sakes.

4. **No slide hogging.** Once your kid is down the slide, make her go back around and up the ladder before her next trip. No stopping at the bottom and scaling back up the slope of the slide while the two-year-old patiently waiting his turn at the top starts to weep. This rule also calls for the rapid removal of any toddler who gets cold feet and sits frozen in panic while a growing chorus of whines emanates from the ladder behind him.

5. **Obey the laws of the sandbox.**

   - **No sand throwing.** Don't let your kid toss the stuff around into the faces of other tots: Remember what happened to the guy who kicked sand in the face of the teen in the old Charles Atlas comic book ads.

   - **The sandbox is not a litter box.** By now, you should begin to recognize the facial expressions and body language that accompany your child's excretory excursions. If you see those signs, hustle the kid to higher ground.

   - **If it's left in the sandbox, it belongs to the sandbox.** If there's a toy that your child is so attached to that she will be devastated upon losing it, don't let her take it to the playground—and most importantly, don't let her take it into the sandbox. The sand consumes toys of all kinds, and when playthings are lost to the sand, they become fair game for any junior archaeologist who comes along to dig them up. So if your daughter spots some little boy playing with the Polly Pocket she lost four weeks earlier, you cannot demand its return.

avoiding conflict altogether. But the mother's complete disregard for the safety of all the pre-preschoolers playing innocently around her incited me to action. I walked over to her and politely asked her to curb her child's behavior, hoping that she was one of those parents who is often embarrassed by her abnormally rowdy child, and that she would be profusely apologetic.

That was not the case. She laid into me with a venomous Sue Hawk–like tirade that I could still hear in the distance even once Bryn and I had fled far beyond the playground gates.

The most frustrating aspect of that whole incident was not the egregious behavior of that harpy or her beastling, but the fact that none of the other parents backed me up. There were several other toddlers in just as much danger of getting a bonk on the head as Bryn. I even noticed some of the parents gasping whenever the boy from the Dark Side got too close to their kids. But when I chose to act, they all left me standing like Gary Cooper at the end of *High Noon.* Had the other parents joined me in a coalition, we probably would have been able to oust that tyrant—but instead, I had to convince my two-year-old that a walk in the park would be more fun than the sandbox. None of this would have been an issue at all, of course, if the villain of this vignette had followed some simple rules for playground etiquette.

PART IV

THE (RUG)RAT RACE: WORK AND HOME

Here we go with another of those hot-button topics that parents like to debate with foaming-at-the-mouth ferocity. When it comes to choosing between remaining at home with the baby or going back to work, though, only you and your wife can determine what's best for your family. Being a stay-at-home parent hardly means you're tossing away any future ambitions in favor of, say, crafting construction-paper bats to hang outside your house on Halloween. Nor does your part in a two-income couple guarantee children who would fail to recognize you in a lineup.

But whichever decision you make, other questions will follow: If you and your spouse both work, who will watch the baby? If you're home alone all day with the baby, will you find anyone to converse with who has the power of speech? Whether you spend your days behind a desk or at a changing table, it's certainly not going to be business as usual.

CHAPTER 8

Men at Work

Let's start off by acknowledging a truism: Mothers have it worse. When women rejoin the workforce after having a baby, they face an untold number of Guilt Snipers taking potshots at them from the pages of newsmagazines and the rambling rants of talk radio. As men, we can't claim to fully understand the complexities of being a twenty-first-century working mother.

Having established that, let's look at how much it can suck to be a working dad.

WORKING DADS NEED LOVE, TOO

Those of us with kids are putting in longer hours than ever before—the average American father now clocks in a fifty-one-hour work-week. If you're among the men who do, I *suppose* you could be in it just for the daily ten hours away from your wife and child. But you probably hold down a job for more pragmatic reasons, like money, health insurance, or a tax-free dependent care account. Or, hey, maybe it's because you actually have interests outside your family. Either way, your choice to work is not an indication that you only care about your baby as much as you would some kind of hamster-like disposable pet.

There is a reason, though, why "Daddy Guilt" is not a term you hear thrown around very often. As a man, you are *expected* to continue working, so when you do, no one ever implies you're choosing career over family.

But this doesn't mean you won't start resenting your job, if it starts co-opting too much of your time and attention. This can be especially true if the position you're currently holding isn't exactly on the thrilling, I'm-going-to-change-the-world career track you once envisioned for yourself back at cap-and-gown time. Even if you love what you do for a living, you can still be stricken by regret every time your mind wanders from the task at hand and you start imagining all the wonderful, amazing things you just know your child must be doing in your absence.

> "For the first three years of my son's life, I was working free-lance from home, so he was used to always having me around. I just recently started a full-time job, and truth be told, I really do feel guilty. I rationalize it by reminding myself that this is the way most of the world does it. But it still hurts to hear that sometimes when my wife takes him home from the cooperative day school we have him in, he asks, 'Is Daddy gonna be there?'"
> —Peter R., Brooklyn, NY

In a big-picture sense, things are gradually improving for those men who care about their children as well as the contents of their briefcases. Employers around the country have increasingly begun to offer paid paternity leave (although "increasingly" still doesn't add up to a very large number) and the Family Medical Leave Act guarantees women *and* men the same right to take twelve weeks off without putting their job in jeopardy (though this law applies only to people employed by companies of fifty people or more and doesn't guarantee any kind of pay). Unfortunately, only an itsy-bitsy percentage of the dads who are eligible for these benefits make use of them. Overall, we're still working in an office culture where logging in enough overtime to forget your child's name is the best way to ensure a chance at a promotion.

"Everyone at my job is very career driven," said one New England dad. "My coworkers actually think I'm lucky that my baby will be with family while my wife and I both work, because I'll be able to 'keep my career moving.' In reality, I'd much rather be home with my child."

One New York dad voiced a common source of discontent among working dads, namely, days that drag on beyond regular nine-to-five hours. "I couldn't imagine not working," he said, "but if I ever have to stay late, I really miss my son. If there's a night I come home and he's already in bed, I feel a terrible sense of loss."

If you and your wife both used to work, but now she's going to be staying home with the baby, you've also got to adjust to being the family's sole breadwinner. That's an awful lot of extra responsibility. And it's exactly the kind of pressure that may make you feel compelled to work later, longer, and harder—and end up leaving "Take Your Children to Work Day" as the only opportunity for you to see your kid. But before anybody starts singing "Cat's in the Cradle," there are pluses to being a working father.

For one thing, if your superiors have children of their own, the fact that you now have something in common can bring about a sudden surge in their esteem for you. One dad told me that prior to the birth of his daughter, he was just one of many nameless peons at work; but as soon as he had a baby, he was on the boss's radar and became the big man's go-to guy for parenting talk.

Time with a baby can also function as de facto leadership training, bestowing you with new skills that you might start uncon-
sciously implementing at work. Before you know it, you're a better
communicator, speaking to appreciative office mates in the same
slow, clear manner you use with your baby. You're listening better,
too, finding it easier to understand the ideas of coworkers who can't
express themselves very well. You may even discover that you have
more patience with whiny coworkers (though I don't suggest that
you pat them on the head, shush them, and sing to them until they
calm down).

EMPLOYEE HANDBOOK: HOW TO BE A WORKING DAD WITHOUT FREAKING OUT YOUR COLLEAGUES

Working dads have far more to think about than just changing the number
of exemptions on their tax forms. Aside from the obvious challenge posed by
performing on less sleep and with a newly split focus, you must not forget
the smaller details that will help to shape your colleagues' opinions of you.

- **Phoning Home:** Speaking to your child over the phone in earshot of others is a challenge all of us must face. Most people will understand and accept the professions of love you will speak into the receiver (though it
might be better to append every "I love you" with the child's name, to
clarify the situation for any eavesdroppers). They may even give you a pass
on your use of the third person (e.g., "Daddy will fix your squeaky duck as
soon as Daddy gets home"). However, you should not expect anybody—
your child, included—to tolerate cutesy-wootsey, oogy-boogy, googly-
woogly talk. Save that for behind closed doors. Or better yet, put the ki-
bosh on it all together and let your baby learn some real words.

- **Baby Shrines:** No one should deny you a few tasteful photographs of
your child for your work area. Knowing you're a parent, it might even

strike a few people as odd if they *don't* see a JPEG of a pudgy-faced infant on your computer desktop. The occasional crayon scribbling taped to your wall is usually also acceptable—and, as a bonus, explaining that the squiggles on the paper are supposed to be you riding a flying giraffe can fill those awkward silences whenever someone whose name you can't remember stops by to fill your in-box. There's a big difference, though, between being a proud father and ostentatiously flaunting your parenthood. If there are more baby pictures than work-related materials on your desk, people might start thinking, "Unhealthy obsession."

And be sure to steer clear of photos that feature you in any state of undress, even tasteful black-and-white portraits of a shirtless you cradling your newborn like the models in those wholesomely erotic posters that hang in every college girl's dorm room.

- **Leaving the Baby at Home:** Whereas, in the past, you may have had trouble leaving your work at the office, you may now find yourself struggling with the inverse of that equation. You talk and act differently around a baby than you do around other adults; sometimes it can be hard to switch gears when you need to. I still find it virtually impossible to end a conversation with anything other than a pert "bye-bye!" But that's a minor infraction. I have heard from—and personally encountered—grown men who start spelling out random words as if there were a child present ("Tad in accounting can be such a j-e-r-k"). And then there's the ultimate (and entirely true) mortification scenario: the parent who stepped out of a business meeting by unthinkingly announcing, "I have to go potty now."

HOW I LEARNED TO STOP WORRYING AND LOVE THE DOUBLE STANDARD

Here's the sad truth: Mothers have their work performance judged far more harshly than women without children, while fathers hear, "*Eh,* you've got a kid now; we can't possibly expect your work to meet anything resembling an acceptable standard anymore." According to a December 2004 study in *The Journal of Social Issues,* people have lower expectations of working dads than they do *any* other group—that includes not only guys without kids but working mothers as well. What does this mean for you? You can get away with a lot of crap you couldn't before!

Before I go any further, this double standard is completely unfair; ideally, companies would give a little wiggle room to working parents of both genders. However, the fact that you may often be given the benefit of the doubt on the job can tempt you to abuse this little ethics loophole. It would be so easy; your child provides you with an instant exit strategy ("I'm afraid I'm gonna have to miss the meeting this afternoon; Jenny's got a fever again," "I'd love to put in some overtime with the rest of you guys, but my wife's out of town and I have to pick up the kids"). Children also make perfectly convenient scapegoats ("I just couldn't finish that report with the baby screaming all night," "Sorry I'm late; diaper blowout"). Perhaps you have files that you can't turn in because they got finger-paint smudges on them, or maybe you lost your passcard because "the baby must have snatched it"—little children are capable of almost anything.

"Kids are a brilliant alibi," said one California dad. "But in my defense, if I claim I have kid stuff to do, I really do go and spend time with the kids, rather than just sneak over to the nearest Starbucks."

If you're not a paragon of honesty, you could try to justify this behavior by telling yourself you're sticking it to The Man and his bias-ridden American workplace. Just be careful you don't overplay your bid for sympathy or you'll end up well-deserving of any scorn your coworkers find it in their hearts to throw your way ("There he goes, leaving early again—you know, my cat threw up this morning, but you don't see me rushing for the door").

Plus, you don't want to become The Boy Who Cried Ear Infection. Use your kid as a "Get Out of Jail Free" card too often and your superiors may finally decide to bring down the gavel on an occasion when you genuinely *need* to be excused. And that may leave you having to choose between the wrath of your boss or that of a child-care provider who desperately wants your phlegm-hacking toddler away from her healthier charges.

The main thing we need to avoid is giving disgruntled anti-child staffers a way to claim the moral high ground. Many "childfree" people like to imply that you are unjustly receiving preferential treatment if you are given permission to dash out of work early one day to retrieve your sick child from preschool. On the surface, they have a point—you are let off the hook for certain things they might not be. What these folks never take into account is the fact that with family taking up a good part of your energy and attention, you have to work twice as hard to make an impression and move ahead in your career—which makes it all the more satisfying any time you can manage to pass over one of those serial complainers.

CHAPTER 9

Homeward Bound

"Don't ever ask a father if he's babysitting. That's the worst thing you can say to a dad."   —Dave W., Stillwater, MN

If someone in your household is going to be a stay-at-home parent, the big question is: Who? Since we no longer live in TV Land sitcoms, the answer for most couples is based on economics. If your wife's name is regularly bandied about in *The Wall Street Journal,* she's probably the better choice to keep her career track uninterrupted—even if the shoe store manager recently lauded you with rave reviews for the window painting of sledding squirrels you created for his "Snow-tacular Winter Boot Sale."

So let's say you decide to become an at-home dad. Chances are you're taking on that role because you and your wife strongly believe in keeping your baby out of child care. Ha-ha—joke's on you! *You* are child care! At least, you are according to the National Institute of Child Health and Human Development, the government's largest scientific body devoted to research in such areas. Since the early 1990s, the NICHD has been undertaking the world's largest-ever study into the effects of child care upon the very young. The study defines "child care" as any nonmaternal care, including "centers, child-care homes, in-home sitters, grandparents, and fathers."

So there you have it. According to the U.S. Department of Health and Human Services, when it comes to watching your own kid, you should be lumped in with sixteen-year-olds looking for summer jobs that don't involve grease burns, and all fifty-eight nameless employees at your local franchise of KidKare, Inc. To be fair, the study has found that babies in father-care benefit because of the much better child-to-caregiver ratio than those in large day-care centers—although, when compared with the staff members at those big centers, fathers tend to rank much lower in "specialized training in child development" and "years of child-care experience."

While that sinks in, let's try to answer the most common question you will hear as a stay-at-home-dad:

SO WHAT DO YOU DO ALL DAY?

Being a stay-at-home parent in the early months has its pros and cons. On the plus side, the baby is relatively immobile, sleeps a lot, and can't get into too much trouble. The negative: She's not great company. I've heard more parents than I can count say, "There's no one I'd rather spend time with than my child." But I'm pretty sure they weren't talking about a two-month-old baby. As the stay-at-home parent of a newborn, you'll spend your day not so much doing things *with* the baby, as doing things while holding the baby. Whenever your day isn't physically draining (from, say, trying to vacuum one-handed while balancing an infant in the crook of your other elbow), it will be psychologically challenging (as when you can't move a muscle for fear of waking the sleeping baby on your chest and you realize the TV is tuned to QVC with no remote in sight).

Often the bulk of the household chores fall to the stay-at-home parent. "Whoever stays home with the kids, whether it's the father or the mother, can't expect the other person to take on a full 50 percent of the housework," said Dave Weiss, who heads up the Minnesota Dads At Home network. "After my wife comes home from a long day at work, she only has maybe two or three hours with the kids before their bedtime—she's not going to wash ten loads of laundry, cut the lawn, and paint the shed. Sure we're both tired at the end of the day, but it's a different kind of tired."

At least the stay-at-home dad usually has his wife around on maternity leave through the first six weeks or more, which can help ease him through the transition. After the first few months, as your baby becomes increasingly active—and more importantly, interactive—your relationship will go from just, "Everything's okay, baby; Daddy's got your bottle for you," to include, "Great job, now you push the truck back to me!"

In time, your baby can become your playmate, as opposed to just your responsibility. A momentous turning point occurs when your kid starts to understand what you're saying, and you can finally stop feeling like Tom Hanks chatting with Wilson the soccer ball in *Cast Away*. But having a child to keep you company all day doesn't diminish your need for adult contact. Of the two biggest problems facing at-home dads, the one most mentioned to me was the isolation, the terrible soul-crushing isolation.

"The solitude really got to me," said Eric H. of Mechanicsville, Virginia. "I hit a point where telemarketers would call, and I'd be, 'Hey, how are you doing?'" To find salvation, he took the same route so many other at-home dads try: joining a dads group (see Chapter 10).

Aside from the loneliness, the other complaint I repeatedly heard: "People just don't get it." The guys were referring not only to those folks who don't understand the amount of work that goes into being an at-home parent, but also to the ones who find it hard to believe that a man would actually want to take on such a role. "My grandfather still thinks I've been on vacation from work this whole time," said one stay-at-homer. Another told me that his mother-in-law likes to leave clipped-out "help wanted" ads on his kitchen table. But there are lots of guys who stay at home and really like it. I've heard dads speak about the rush of pride they feel upon discovering parenting acumen they didn't know they possessed, the gratitude they have for the close parent-child relationship that might never have developed under other circumstances, and the guilty pleasure of playing with toys again.

"My biggest fear is that my wife will realize how much fun I have doing this," said one dad. "Because if she does, *she'll* want to stay home."

RETURN OF THE MOTHER

Being with the baby all day will allow you to put your stamp on his evolving personality—although that's something which doesn't always go over so well with the working parent.

By spending so much time with your child, you're bound to develop your own personal techniques for feeding, bathing, dressing, and the like. And you will become territorial about those tasks. Then, when your wife is home on evenings and weekends, she's probably going to pitch in and take over a number of the baby-related chores to give you a break. She's not, however, going to check in with you for instructions.

Suddenly, you're hectoring your spouse with comments like, "You can't give him *just* peas—he likes them mixed with the winter squash," or "No, no, no—he never takes his nap without Blinky

Bunny." And she's firing back with, "Just because I work all day doesn't mean I don't know how to be a mother." Obviously not ideal.

To avoid that, both you and your spouse need to look at each situation through the other's bloodshot eyes. It can be incredibly frustrating for her to feel like some stranger auditing your detailed parenting curriculum. But it can also be a blow for you to see her stroll in and do things her own way—especially if her methods work just as well as yours.

Take this from someone who has been on both sides of the equation. When my wife was home with our daughter in the first few months while I schlepped to the office, it was hard not to be irked by an innocent comment from her about how I might want to try holding the baby in a different way (I believe parenthood may literally decrease the thickness of one's skin by at least several millimeters). After we switched places, with my wife taking on a new job and me becoming the at-home parent, I felt the sting of seeing that even when my wife eschewed the bouncing-spoon-accompanied-by-chomping-sound-effect technique I had implemented for feeding time, the baby devoured her sweet potato mush just as voraciously. And after Bryn entered day care, my wife and I both became acquainted with that mix of pride and heartbreak you get each time your child performs some new activity, like counting backward, that you know neither of you taught her.

Another big source of conflict: Who plays parent in the evening? More than a few stay-at-home dads said to me, "I love being with my kids all day, but when their mom comes home, I can't wait to pass them off to her."

To see things from the other side, here's what one working dad had to say about the pressure he felt from being the parent who receives that handoff: "The second I get home, my wife wants me to take complete responsibility for the baby. I know she's been working hard all day, but I've been working, too. A lot of times, I'm exhausted. I believe that when I come home, it should be time for us to share the parenting, not 'Dad's home, so now it's Mom's free time.'"

Sharing makes sense. The stay-at-home parent definitely needs a breather after endless hours of nothing but baby, baby, baby. And the working parent—especially those who spend their days, say, jackhammering or teaching martial-arts classes—may legitimately be too worn out to take over for the entirety of the evening. But the biggest reason why the two of you should share parenting at the end of the day is because, during the week, that time may be your only real chance to share it. After all, you probably only have a couple of hours between the end of the workday and bedtime during which you and your spouse can interact with your child together.

That's why in many families Mom and Dad both show up for baby's evening bath—something which certainly does not need to be a group activity. My wife and I regularly tag-team Bryn's longer-than-necessary bedtime ritual of books, songs, and stories. While one of us is reading *Madeline in London* or singing "Edelweiss," the other is generally lying down—resting and participating simultaneously.

CHAPTER 10

In the Company of Men

Dads groups can be oases of adult companionship in the "all-children, all the time" life of a stay-at-homer. But they can serve a purpose for working fathers, too: When childless friends have grown tired of hearing about Boppys and Binkys, these fatherhood connection hubs also offer a social outlet in which you can initiate a discussion about glow-in-the-dark diapers without fearing ostracism. And for those of you not keen on mingling, there are always Internet-based groups (in fact, you'll probably have to use the Web to find a live group, too—check local community sites, fatherhood Web rings, or stay-at-home dad hubs such as Slowlane.com). Both the online and in-person versions offer a safe haven in which you can feel free to ask otherwise embarrassing questions.

So, go ahead, come straight out with, "What's the longest you've ever gone without realizing your son was sitting in his own feces?" That's the glory of a dads group.

MIX AND MATCH: Dads Group Open Admissions

If you're the type of guy who spends his free time analyzing the Truffaut canon, you might be able to work amicably with a colleague whose main pastime is the sports trivia machine at Houlihan's, but you probably aren't looking to hang out with him on weekends. Yet this is exactly what people do in a dads group.

"Oh, I know for a fact that I wouldn't be caught dead talking to some of these guys in the real world," one attendee told me. "But here I have a good time with them."

"If I tried, I probably couldn't find a bunch of guys who I have less in common with," said another. "Yet I look forward to seeing them every week."

This defies everything we ever learned about socialization in high school: The members of the chess club didn't get together *just* to shift around pawns and bishops, they also knew they had a good likelihood of finding another person there with whom they could discuss the latest issue of *Green Lantern*. Back then, time was too precious to waste with anyone who didn't share at least 97 percent of your interests. And while it's true that most men mature quite a bit in the years between mortarboard and Baby Björn, devoting your free time to a bunch of guys with whom you have only one thing in common still sounds a bit risky. Every guy at a dads group is betting pretty heavily that the shared experience of fatherhood will be enough to make them want to keep seeing one another. Miraculously, it often seems to work.

You can meet any or all of the following types in your dads group. Will you be able to make nice with all of them?

- **The Marathoner:** He hikes eight miles to and from the meeting with twins strapped to his back. His recounting of last weekend's hiking trip is infused with the moaning sensuality of a Barry White single. You hear him repeatedly have to say, "Sorry, sweetie, the Tiger's Milk bar is just for Daddy."

- **The Ponytail:** He supplies the carob-chip spelt cookies for each get-together. Whatever your ailment, he can suggest an herb. He hums James Taylor.

- **The Clavin:** He will spout off questionable trivia at any given opportunity ("Did you know that babies are 98 percent water?"). He is unnaturally quick to go on the defensive if any of his unsolicited factoids are questioned ("Well, don't blame me if the Discovery Health Channel got it wrong"). Each time he sees you, he acts as if he's forgotten how awkward your previous encounter was.

- **BlackBerry Man:** He refers to his car by model. His clothes are cleaner than they should be for a man with a child that young. At least once per session, you have to run to retrieve his toddler from down the hall while he's text messaging.

- **The Self-Described Rebel:** He shows how counterculture he is by wearing T-shirts from bands whose names alone carry "parental advisory" stickers. He frequently mentions how he can't wait until he can finally take his kid to Austin. His child's name (and possibly, portrait) is tattooed somewhere on his body.

- **The One-Man Baby Bazaar:** He comes equipped with enough child-care gear to run a professional nursery. He has more pockets than the entire men's department of an Old Navy store. His sales pitches will make you wonder if he's getting kickbacks from baby-goods companies ("Check out this new bottle from Dr. Brown's. This puppy's got streamlined natural-flow action. Go ahead, take a sip; see how it feels").

- **The Disgruntled Husband:** Whether he says so or not, it's obvious his wife made him go. He has a tendency for moping. When moved to speak, it will often be to question the nature of the group ("So what is this supposed to be, anyway, some kind of class?").

WHY DO WE ALL JUST GET ALONG?

It was at my first dads group—when I saw Bryn crawling around and her peers stepping gracefully over her—that I realized my daughter was a late walker. However, any anxiety I felt about this point was entirely internal; none of the other guys made note of the fact that their kids were practically turning pirouettes while mine had to cling to the back of a chair just to remain upright for a few seconds. In a place that you might assume would be a petri dish for the One-upmanship Virus, you're likely to see surprisingly little grandstanding. With the exception of the occasional random jerk, dads groupers tend to rein in fatherly bravado, and are not likely to pull out a bullhorn every time their baby pulls off some minor feat.

Perhaps it's the *un*natural nature of these groups—the inherent lack of depth in these relationships—that keeps things mellow. Fatherhood alone brought all these guys here; no one wants to dribble a drop of verbal acid on the one thread that's holding the entire gang together. "At the group, the guys will overlook just about everything for the kids," said Jason K., who heads a group in Milwaukee. "The kids are the glue. Without that connection, you don't have these other guys to talk to and ask questions to. And how else can you find out if what you're doing with your kid is right or not?"

> "Our group is not just a bunch of knuckle-draggin' monkeys looking to kill time until our wives get home. Well, sometimes we are, but that's beside the point. Most often, we're looking for practical advice on how to handle something that has become an issue for us."
> —Chad N., Austin, TX

"At my dads group, the conversations were all about strollers and bottles," said one New York dad. "These guys were strictly there to share information about their kids. They took their jobs as dads very seriously: no football talk."

A case can be made that it is the more business-minded groups that stay around longer. When members attempt to get chummy, that's when the forced nature of the grouping can become painfully apparent. At one of the groups I attended, a member brought up his Australian vacation and soon everyone was engaged in travel talk. It was great; I'm interested in geography and foreign cultures—no problem. Then, with a non sequitur that must have slipped right past me, the conversation switched to the NCAA. Though I have never watched an hour of college basketball in my life, I kept chiming in for fear of being the last one picked in the event that these guys decided to kick up a game after the meeting. Fortunately, I was able to fake my way through the discussion gracefully (mostly by commenting on mascots). But I was treading dangerous ground: Sports is one of those topics that can get certain men diving for one another's throats. If I had inadvertently insulted someone's favorite team, I could have ended up finding myself in a sprint for safety—my startled and confused daughter tucked under my arm—as a mob of angry fans hunted me down like Piggy in *Lord of the Flies.*

Confining all group dialogue to baby-centric topics is a fine way of avoiding such incidents. But for many groupers, there's a real desire for conversation that goes beyond soy-formula testimonials. This is especially true of any stay-at-home dads in the group for whom the meetings may be their only opportunity for nonrelative contact. In most cases—especially if the gang's been together for a long time and all cradle cap discussions have run their course—the guys will want to talk about other things. That's when luck (as opposed to the children) becomes the main factor in whether or not a group remains intact. Because when the conversation shifts out of baby land, all bets are off.

After all, we are men: Do we not have fiery tempers and unwavering opinions? Well, some of us do. This is why many groups set ground rules for conversation: Controversial topics are off-limits.

But what of the guy who can't sleep at night without expressing just how incensed he was by his group-mate's "Nader in '08" button? For him, there's always the Internet.

NOTHING BUT NET: Dads on the Web

"We pretty much ban political and religious discussion from the group meetings, but we have Internet message boards where the guys can go and argue all they want. It can get pretty fierce," explained a grouper in Virginia. "What I'm always left thinking, though, is where the heck do they find the time to write all this stuff?"

Some men have the remarkable ability to engage in online name-calling with their ideological opposites and then put their vitriol to sleep with their computers, leaving nothing but good-natured joshing for the next time they see their virtual nemeses in person at a group meeting. But how long can someone keep that up? If there's an issue that gets you riled up enough to compose broadsides about it, pretending to get along with a guy who you know scoffs at your beliefs has *got* to start eating away at your stomach lining—no matter how much you want to keep up a good public face. I think this every time I see a press photo of Bush and Clinton hugging each other at some foreign dignitary's birthday party.

If you doubt your capacity to make nice with your ideological enemies, logging on to one of the many Internet-only dads groups can be

A MAN AMONG WOMEN: THE DANGERS OF MIXED COMPANY

It's possible you may be thinking about enlisting in a unisex playgroup. Maybe you're the type of guy who always had more female than male friends. Maybe *Iron John* has forever tainted your idea of all-male gatherings. Or maybe there are just no dads groups in your neighborhood. Whatever the reason, if you do enter such a situation, do so knowing that "unisex" in this context often means "women's" with an asterisk.

There are a few possible pitfalls you should keep in mind. If you're the gender outsider, you may be greeted with any of the following:

- **Assumed incompetence.** "When we go to ballet class, since I'm the only man there, if my kid misbehaves, that's because 'Oh, it's the *guy's* kid.'"— Pat C., Chicago, IL
- **Distrust.** "It's frustrating, but a lot of women just aren't comfortable having a strange man around their kids. I'm a guy with a beard. That doubles the problem."—Andrew B., Milwaukee, WI
- **Feigned acceptance.** "At Gymboree, it was all moms . . . and me. I was uncomfortable, so I asked if me being there would be a problem. They said no, of course. But it was obvious the women wanted to bond amongst themselves. I mostly just played with the kids."—Michael A., Los Angeles, CA
- **Too much acceptance.** "I've become one of the girls to them. They forget I'm a man; I'm just someone else who's there. But I don't want to hear about periods all the time."—Richard S., Atlanta, GA

an appealing option—just as it is for shy, distrustful, or incredibly unhygienic men. But perhaps the two things that most help online dads groups to flourish are time and geography. I heard from numerous guys who said they either left a dads group or couldn't join one to begin with because the meetings weren't local. With the click of a mouse obviously being preferable to a long commute, we should be thankful we live in an age when one can telecommute for male bonding.

Throughout the writing of this book, I've followed the goings on at several fatherhood message boards. It's amazing how much more honest and open guys are with one another in an online forum than when the dudes they're speaking to can look them in the eyes. Men recommend baby shampoos with impunity. They admit to crying, without disclaimers about how they normally never shed a tear.

"Guys don't talk to one another like women do, and sometimes we just need a place to vent," said Roger, moderator of the Yahoo! Expectant and New Dads Club. It's not hard at all to find your own online band of brothers—provided you can learn to type with a baby on your lap (an activity that is frequently discussed on such boards).

While forging long-lasting friendships is typically not the main goal of joining any dads group, the near impossibility of forming such a bond online is the biggest downside to Internet communities. With face-to-face gatherings, at least you've got the long-shot chance that fate could land you in the same group as a future best friend.

"In the first year, the online relationships are probably more valuable in terms of combating isolation," said Casey S. of Sacramento, California. "But you have to look to live groups for spin-off value. If you find even one good friend there that you end up seeing on the outside, you're set."

CHAPTER 11

Someone to Watch Over Them

Nanny or day care? Your place or theirs? It's a tough call for a lot of parents: With individual care, there's no fear of your baby becoming known as "the one with the curly hair," while in a group situation, you can be pretty sure you won't end up with a spoiled kid accustomed to having a personal assistant at his every beck and call. The National Institute of Child Health and Human Development likes to split the difference; their studies have shown that infants benefit from individual care and toddlers fare better in group care. At the same time, the agency stresses the importance of stability and says there could be detrimental effects from changing caregivers. So you're screwed either way.

ON YOUR TURF

I'm not sure exactly when our culture became obsessed with nannies. But these women are no longer hired just by the grotesquely rich alongside chambermaids and personal chefs. For middle-income families in search of child care, nannies are now automatically in the mix. And the ones that we know and love from the past wouldn't even get a second interview nowadays: Mary Poppins hung out with chimney sweeps; do you really think she had a college education, let alone a degree in child development? Today's full-time babysitters often come equipped with lengthy résumés and more certifications than your average neurosurgeon. Ask to see her qualifications and she might pull out papers attesting to her competence in everything from CPR and first aid to "physical management of aggressive behavior."

It makes sense, given the current state of parental anxiety: When child care has become such a specific science, how can we trust anyone other than a qualified expert? We can't even trust ourselves, it seems—which is why we've seen the appearance of a multitude of Barnum-esque entrepreneurs who sell themselves as "parenting coaches" and charge exorbitant amounts of money to be on call for emergency questions about diaper rash. TV shows like *Supernanny* and *Nanny 911* have pit incompetent parents against omnipotent professional caregivers. It only follows that these phenoms are the ones we'd *want* in charge of our kids.

Of course, those people are the most expensive—so many of us reluctantly hire recent college grads looking to kill time until they kick off their "real careers." Or immigrant women willing to work off-the-books until they can someday be reunited with their own families back in their homelands.

When it comes to hiring a nanny, you know to check her references, consider her experience, yada yada. But what you're really looking for, dads say, is someone you can trust—and not just with the baby.

1. Can You Trust Her with Your Stuff?
Someone's going to be unsupervised in your home for several hours: Quick, what needs to be hidden? As a rule, nothing giggle-worthy should be left in clear—or easily uncovered—view. This includes everything from tubes of Astroglide to Pokémon Game Boy car-

tridges that obviously don't belong to your nine-month-old. One dad told me about an old stack of girlie magazines that remains untouched in his closet, except for those times after the nanny leaves, when he feels the compulsive need to check and make sure they're still sitting in that same place he stashed them years earlier.

Some guys go overboard with secreting away various household items and bits of information. Gin bottles will be stowed away on high closet shelves, and bank statements will be tucked into the pages of boring-sounding books. This is really more work than you need to do, though. If your babysitter would contemplate hitting the booze while on duty, you've got bigger problems than the relative ease with which she can obtain access to your own personal stash of hooch. And if the person you've hired is a criminal, she'll be rifling through all your drawers anyway; leaving a checkbook on your desk is not going to tempt a previously law-abiding citizen into a life of information thievery. A few calls to her previous employers might do better to ease your mind than turning your home into a continuous scavenger hunt.

Still paranoid about your kid, your MP3 player, the quarters in your spare change jar? You can always go the hidden camera route. The use of the nanny-cam is rife with controversy, but what's a little ethical dilemma compared to the assurance that your sitter isn't plopping your baby in front of eight hours of Nick Jr. while she ducks into the bathroom to reenact scenes from *Trainspotting*. Whatever peace of mind a surveillance system brings, it also comes with the possibility of losing a good sitter if she finds out she's been secretly recorded. There's also the chance that you yourself might be breaking any number of state laws (check with a lawyer before you install a Web-cam in the plastic eyeballs of Chicken Dance Elmo).

And be realistic: Are you going to take the time every day to sit and review what must be some incredibly dull videos?

2. Can You Trust Her Not to Leave?

If you decide to fork over all sorts of referral fees to a nanny agency—or even to hire your caregiver straight from a governess school (yes, you can do that, and yes, there are governess schools)—you can probably rest assured that the woman you hire is thinking of her position with you as a long-term appointment. Take any other route—say, a neighborhood bulletin-board posting, fringed with tear-off phone numbers, that boldly declares "I WILL WATCH YOUR CHILDREN!"— and you can't be so sure.

Despite a lack of experience, a younger nanny who is new to the workforce may be less apt to tinker with the rules you set out for her. Since she's still learning herself, she's unlikely to become Miss Bossy-Pants and insist she knows better (a possible problem with sitters who've been around the crib a few times already). An eager and earnest young nanny may be just the person you're looking for. However, the moment any offer of a better position comes in, she may drop you like a deodorant-phobic blind date. Make sure you find out up front if your nanny is considering sitterhood as just an "in-between" stage until DreamWorks options her blog.

"I was devastated when our nanny quit," said one New York dad. "It felt like a breakup, like I'd just been dumped."

There are no guarantees, of course: Virtually any nanny can be wooed away by offers of better pay or benefits. Or, if she's been at the baby biz for a long time, she might at some point look to try some other line of work, or even retire. So, if you want your nanny to stick around: incentives, incentives, incentives.

3. Can You Trust Her with Your Wife?

To the Howard Stern fans out there, no, that's not what I'm talking about. A lot of women have been known to bond with their nannies; I've known a few who broke down and wept when their caregiver left the job. While a dad can become friendly with his nanny (if not Jude Law–friendly), it's usually nothing like the intensity of the sisterhood his wife may forge with her. Between the shared experience of child rearing and a mother's desire to maintain a deeper connection to her baby by staying close to his caregiver, a wife and a nanny can get pretty tight. And husbands have been known to get jealous. I've heard men say they felt supplanted by their child's sitter. At a time in a marriage when a wife's attention is already divided between husband and baby, it's not hard for some guys to feel uneasy with the idea of someone new jumping in for a share.

Looking at the situation pragmatically, though, a nanny who is on "best friend" terms with your wife is a lot less likely to ditch your family for employers who'll pay her fifty cents more per hour. Question #2 taken care of.

4. Can You Trust Yourself to Be a Good Employer?

The whole employer-employee relationship can make a nanny situation uncomfortable for a lot of people. I've heard many parents attest to their full-time sitter being "like part of the family." As great as such a development can be for the kids, it can make a lot of dads uncomfortable if they can only pay their new "family member" minimum wage with no health benefits.

"Our son absolutely loved our nanny, and I really grew to like her as a person myself," said one East Coast father. "But when my wife and I started becoming closer to her, the fact that she was a minimum-wage employee really struck me hard. It just didn't feel right. We couldn't afford to pay her any more than we were, so we helped her find a better-paying gig with another family."

HELP WANTED (NO MEN NEED APPLY)

Notice how I've been using "her" to refer to the caregiver through this whole chapter? There's a reason.

I attended a rather ingenious five-minute interview marathon event in Manhattan set up by the national referral service Sittercity. It was sort of like speed-dating for nannies. Parents worked their way around a room full of potential child-care providers, asking as many questions as they wanted for five minutes; after a bell rang, they would move down the line to the next hopeful. As soon as I entered the room, in which fifty or so hirable sitters filled out a huge semicircle of desks, I noticed one lone man seated among all the female sitters, and I went straight to him for my first interview. He was a very nice guy in his twenties with a decent-sounding résumé, who seemed eminently competent. I asked him if, since he was the only male caregiver at the event, anybody had asked him any strange questions. His answer was, "Actually, they're all pretty much skipping me."

I don't blame Sittercity for this—after all, the company brought him there for the interview session, which should have offered him ample opportunity for work. I blame the still-pervasive notion that the combination of men and children is good for nothing more than slapstick farce. I blame Vin Diesel in *The Pacifier*. I blame *Two and a Half Men*. We're cutting ourselves off from who-knows-how-many-more child-care options by not considering men. I spoke to dads who belonged to child-care cooperatives (self-formed groups in which members avoid having to pay for sitters by trading turns watching one another's kids) that refused to let fathers do the required sitting if their wives weren't present. At least one guy left such a group because of its restrictions, and another got fed up and forced his collective to change its policy.

Of course, we'd be naive to believe it was simply fear of pratfalls that kept women from putting their children in our care. There's also the horribly offensive assumption that any man who wants to spend time with children might be a sexual predator. I blame Court TV movies for this. I blame local news. And the pedophiles, of course. I blame them, too.

ON THEIR TURF

Day care has gotten a bad rap ever since the eighties, when local newscasts were flooded with stories about a supposed epidemic of Satan worship. To this day, the child-care centers depicted in the media more resemble the Triangle Shirtwaist factory than they do a school of any kind. It's not news when all the kids at a day care come out happy and well adjusted. Odds are, the place you send your child will be fine—just do your research first. And figure out which kind of day care you want for your kid, because there are huge variations. What one parent will look at as a mini-gulag, another will view as "just the kind of structure my little imp needs to get him in shape."

Theoretically, there are a multitude of child-care choices out there for you. But once you take into account their fees, distance from your home, and hours (a whole lot of them end at 3 p.m., negating their use for many two-income families), you'll probably be left with no more than a handful of realistic options. Keeping that in mind, here are a few of the possible child-care situations that you might be stuck choosing from.

1. **The old lady down the block.** Maybe there's some neighborhood fixture who you've known for years as "the lady who watches

people's kids." She's uncertified, but cheap. And dozens of word-of-mouth references from other parents around town may outweigh a piece of paper with the state seal on it, anyway. The day care will take place at her home and probably only include a couple of kids besides yours. She's got decades of experience and the kindhearted demeanor of a Disney grandmother, not to mention the most flexible schedule of all caregivers. Putting your child in her care, though, may mean subjecting him to some seriously outdated beliefs. And chances of your boy getting any computer training are pretty much nil.

2. **The playgroup.** No facades here; the name says it all. You need someone to watch your kid while you're at work, and here is a person who will do just that: Watch. The group is usually run by a stay-at-home mother who said to herself, "While I'm taking care of my own kids, I might as well throw a few more into the mix and make some extra money." As a "professional mom," she'll probably be more likely to get down on the floor and demonstrate her crayon skills for the kids, as well as craft "fun" lunches, like cheese sandwich faces with olive eyes and pickle mouths. This will definitely provide a no-stress environment for your child, but at heart, it's really a playdate: You're just paying for the freedom to leave.

3. **The day school.** Really just a small-scale child-care center; it's a "school" in that the multiple caretakers will lead their charges in enriching activities like tracing one's hand to make a turkey or banging on drums to *Sesame Street Platinum*. But a good portion of the children's day is spent rolling around on foam mats and crawling through nylon tunnels. The owner's "best of both worlds" philosophy features a little bit of education and a whole

lot of interactive play. Fun, sure, but moving on to a real school may feel like a punishment for your kid ("You want me to sit still at this desk? Where are all the bouncy balls? What did I do to deserve this?!").

4. **The big center.** The pinnacle of institutional child care, these sometimes massive buildings are often franchises of national "education companies," and may house several different playrooms for children of different ages. With the number of kids attending, yours should have her pick of many potential friends. Also, there should be no surprises for you, since every bit of information you might need to know will be on the Web site. As a public entity, the place will have a reputation that can be easily verified—one that it wants to keep sparkling. Everything in the center will be extremely well organized and frighteningly clean, although possibly somewhat hospital-like.

5. **The child-care collective.** A bunch of parents, fed up with the lack of what they consider decent options, team up to form their own child-care secessionist movement. Sometimes the cooperative will pool its resources to hire certified teachers, other times it will pull caregivers from among its members. Every parent who brings their child to a collective will be part owner of a daycare center, and as such will have some sort of responsibility toward keeping the school running (door monitor, bake-sale organizer, sawdust bucket duty). By dint of the group's origins, you can be guaranteed a strong ideological bent that, should it mirror yours, will make you feel absolutely secure in your child's treatment during the day. But, well, you have to *work*. And, while not every fringe group is crazy, some are.

6. **Preschool.** Don't you dare call it "day care." For the parent who wants his child to have a bona fide curriculum, this is your choice. Of course, preschools come in various flavors as well:

● **Militant:** when you feel that uniforms, roll call, and assigned seating are the best ways to introduce structure into your child's day. A strict schedule and ultra-specific lesson plan are what lead to a class of two-year-olds on a field trip to the library walking silently down the street in eerily straight lines. They will be very well behaved, but confer a *Village of the Damned*–type apprehension upon all they pass.

● **Artsy:** for staunch believers in teaching through non sequiturs. A "child-directed" approach allows the kids to basically choose the course of study (e.g., one kid likes to play with pots and pans, so instructors lead a cooking lesson; another kid leans toward nose-picking, so instructors bring out books about biology, or possibly spelunking).

● **Pedigree:** because it's never too early to start learning Cantonese. These are the institutions that take the "pre" out of "preschool." Since your toddler will be receiving intensive instruction in all areas of study, he will first need to show the school he's got what it takes. This may mean he'll be subjected to entrance interviews (which I can only assume go something like this: "What assets do you think you can bring to this class, Tommy?" "I saw a bird"). But if he manages to get in, he'll be getting the best preschool education your money can't really buy, but which you can cover with the help of a loan. And by the time he enters kindergarten, your son will kick the ass of any fellow student who dares challenge him to a chess match. Don't worry about the possibility that he might also have a nervous breakdown by the age of seven when he realizes there's no space to list your preschool on most Ivy League college applications.

PART V

WORLDS COLLIDE

Becoming a dad won't change your tastes; if you liked the White Stripes, Jonathan Lethem, or Lost before you had a child, you'll still be into them afterward. However, fatherhood will limit your access to certain elements of entertainment (pile drivers, guitar solos, non-animal nudity), while at the same time, open you up to others (intentionally interactive television, songs that incorporate math, Sneetches). If you cling too tightly to your adult tastes—not only in entertainment, but in personal style and home decor, too—you can begin to suffocate under the avalanche of primary colored plastics. You stand a far greater chance of survival if you are able to find the art-rock dissonance in the tink-tink of a toy piano and invest yourself in the plight of the little bird who mistakenly believes a steam shovel is his mother. Embracing nostalgia while fending off complete regression is difficult, but it's the key to successfully melding your "mature" tastes with the children's pop culture that surrounds you.

CHAPTER 12

Extreme Makeover Home Edition

There will be no hiding the fact that a child lives in your home. It is impossible to limit evidence of the kid's presence to finger paintings on the fridge and a hand-painted wooden sign that has your baby's name spelled out in letter-shaped bugs. It's far more likely that every corner of your residence will hold a reminder of the fact that you are a parent, whether it's some regrettable clown-patterned area rug or one of the small sticky handprints that children use to mark their territory.

PARENTING THROUGH ART DIRECTION:
Setting the Scene for the Perfect Child

Succumbing to the siren call of highly stylized child-goods catalogs is one of the easiest traps for a new dad to fall into. Browsing through page after page of the anal-retentive elegance of Pottery Barn Kids or the postmodern bohemian jubilance of Ikea allows endearingly naive men to believe they can decorate their child's room with furniture and decor that appeals to their own adult aesthetics, while training their children to develop similar tastes in the process.

As a child, I slept with my *Star Wars* comforter for the better part of a decade. Through all those years, nothing made me happier than waking up every morning to the sight of a poorly painted Wookie across my chest. That officially licensed duvet, with its over-crowded starscape of characters and horribly clashing color scheme, was not an item my parents probably found particularly attractive. Yet they, just like the parents of my friends, quietly suffered the whims of a grade-schooler's interior design. My desire for that sci-fi bed set went completely unquestioned.

The bedrooms of today's preschoolers have a decidedly different aesthetic than those of my Hasbro-driven youth. Gone are the Smurf-shaped beanbag chairs and Holly Hobby window treatments. In their stead we see braided chenille rugs, hand-painted boutique lamp shades, and four-poster beds draped with mosquito netting. What happened to those hideous "Hey! I'm sleeping in a Ferrari!" race-car beds that sat in the rooms of every sitcom preteen between 1978 and 1985? Having observed my own child, I feel I can say with some certainty that the tastes of preschoolers have not evolved that much in the past few decades. Yet a company like Garnet Hill can offer a $178 Danish-designed diaper pail and people will buy it.

When you're standing in a children's boutique, staring longingly at a chrome-finish changing table that would look more at home in the Museum of Modern Art than a baby's nursery, you need to ask yourself whether you're about to blow your paycheck on this ex-travagant item because your child would really want it or because you'd prefer it over some lime-green monstrosity covered with bal-loons and butterflies.

Sooner or later you have to face the fact that children have horri-ble taste. And the more your child's belongings spread throughout your house like a nanovirus, the more you may find yourself think-ing, "If I've got to look at this stuff everywhere, at least let it be attractive." That's what leads to the purchase of the $178 designer diaper pail. Save your wallet and your soul by getting creative. One tip suggested by multiple dads: Rotate the toys—not only will you have fewer kiddie things lying around, but the little one's excitement over yesterday's plaything will be rejuvenated after it's been out of circulation for a month.

But really, there's no avoiding your child's stuff. The sheer number of new objects introduced into your home will make organization a Sisyphean task. Preschoolers are like reverse kleptomaniacs, secretly placing random items around the house (a rubber duck in your wife's purse, a MegaBlok in your shoe). Straightening up may need to become a twenty-four-hour chore in order to keep your home from turning into the barricade scene from *Les Misérables*. This is why some men choose the path of least resistance (like the Chicago dad who revealed to me that his coffee table *is* a Thomas the Tank Engine play set, or the California dad who described his house as looking like a Toys "R" Us truck crashed into a Borders bookstore). Choose your battles wisely—please drop any thoughts you might have had of alphabetizing your kid's CDs.

If you do manage to establish a Kid-Free Zone (e.g., "Nothing fluffy on Daddy's desk"), maybe you should also consider making the child's room off-limits from your tastes. Let her have a space of her own for now; there aren't too many years of her life during which she'll be able to—or, for that matter, want to—live in a place that looks like the set of *The Big Comfy Couch*.

"In our master bedroom, there's a cabinet that my daughters have completely cleared out so they can climb around in it. We call it their apartment. Our house is their house, too, and they should have free reign as well." —Bill B., Phoenix, AZ

That thought of giving a kid control over the look of his own room makes a lot of parents cringe, especially the folks who have a very specific vision in mind for their child's space. They want to attempt parenting through art direction. They know that the items we surround ourselves with say a lot about who we are, and when they apply this same concept to children, these parents come to settle rather precariously on the belief that one can mold his child's personality by purchasing the appropriate accoutrements ("But, sir, my daughter couldn't possibly have been the one who started the fight; everything in her room belongs to the same Beatrix Potter theme"). It's quite easy to fall into this line of thinking.

Every company that sells children's products has its own signature aesthetic. At Target, for instance, every lamp, chair, and desk blotter must look like it was designed to be an iMac peripheral. Let's take a look at two case studies that each offer a very specific picture of childhood: Pottery Barn and Ikea.

Skim through any Pottery Barn Kids catalog and you will be amazed by the apparent fact that most grade-schoolers are not only very tidy, but organized to the point of OCD. You're likely to spot checked-off to-do lists in several of the rooms, and every vintage toy and logo-less crayon will be stowed away in its appropriately labeled wicker basket. Children study diligently at their antiqued white desks, they cut out paper dolls, they brush their teeth, they use flash cards, and on Christmas, they sit in their individual monogrammed armchairs and stare at the tree. You can only jump to one conclusion: Stylish, trendy, modern-yet-old-looking furniture creates perfect children.

But what if orderly, intellectual, and urbane is not your idea of the perfect child? The Ikea catalog, in contrast, promises a completely different kind of kid. The Swedish manufacturer's lower price points naturally lend themselves to a more "artist's loft" sensibility. Ikea kids don't just sit quietly and do their homework, they boldly climb across the furniture; they hang from the ceilings; they devour ice-cream cones and let the melting soft-serve drip all over their faces—because they know how to enjoy life, dammit! On the pages of an Ikea catalog you will find children who are creative, free-thinking, and liberally inclusive (each Ikea household appears to be overrun by a multiethnic brood of dreamers). Choosing Ikea means proudly shouting to the world, "It's okay if my child becomes a starving artist! And I'm going to show him that by making sure no two objects in his room are the same color!" An Ikea child would feel stifled and confused in the home of a Pottery Barn kid. Except for the wicker baskets—they both have wicker baskets.

It's not abnormal to want your kids to be like you. But that desire can turn oddly pathological when you want your child to be like your current self, not the way you were at his age. Perhaps I'm fatalistic on this point, but I tend to believe that our children will always thwart our attempts to pigeonhole their personalities while they're young. There's a part of me that knows that no matter how many Shakespearean pop-up books I ply my daughter with, she'll still end up captain of her high school's coed rugby team.

THE SAFETY DANCE

First of all, a little pet peeve of mine: The word "childproofing" is not the correct name for the action it describes. If something is waterproof or fireproof or foolproof, it has been protected from water, fire, or fools, respectively. The term "childproofing" suggests that the intent behind all the locks, gates, and padding with which new parents gussy up their homes is to protect their belongings from the

---

ODE TO THE ALLEN WRENCH

As a dad whose mechanical skills rank only slightly above my ability to squeeze coal into diamonds by hand, I would like to take a moment to offer due praise to the Allen wrench, the magic wand of the shop-class-challenged. Trademarked in 1943 by the Allen Manufacturing Company in Hartford, Connecticut (though said by some to have existed as early as 1911), this little L-shaped hexagonal tube of metal is the reason why I was able to assemble an entire child's-room-worth of furniture with a single tool. Whenever the letters DIY appear in someone's nursery plans, this simplest of implements will save the day.

Thank you, Mr. Allen, wherever you are.

---

kid rather than the other way around. In some instances, like the security latches on the entertainment cabinet, this may be true; but for the most part, we'd like to believe that it is our *children* we intend to keep safe.

"Childproofing," in its most literal sense, is what you do when you visit the home of people who don't have kids of their own, and spend the first twenty minutes of your visit scrambling to remove all of your hosts' ostensibly precious objets d'art to higher ground. Many new fathers lament the unfortunate necessity of this act, wondering why these people, who have knowingly invited a newly mobile baby into their homes, stubbornly refuse even an iota of preparation for their littlest guest. Apparently unaware that toddlers are not very nimble, these folks will blame you for any breakage, rather than their own inability to temporarily shift their Thomas Kinkade collector's plates to a more out-of-reach location.

Fortunately, you have the power to make your *own* home safe for baby. Two-thirds of all injuries to children under three occur in the home (though, of course, home is the place where kids that young spend the vast majority of their time, so it would be far more shocking to hear that most toddler accidents happen at, say, Denny's). Taking certain precautions to prevent such mishaps is only logical. Back in our parents' day, childproofing mostly consisted of yelling, "Stay away from the stairs." Today, you are expected to create a home so secure that Ocean's Eleven couldn't get their hands on the bottle of Febreze barricaded under your sink.

Unlike parents of the sixties and seventies, we don't have to simply trust that our resilient children will shake off the effects of being blasted across a room after jamming their fingers into an electric socket; we have outlet guards. We also have some more dubious safety items, like the refrigerator lock (just how strong *is* your baby?) and the toilet-lid latch (which, when you're in a rush, can lead to a whole different kind of accident).

"If you believed all the stuff about how dangerous life is for babies, and how you're risking eternal grief by not buying the latest titanium-clad, cybertech-enhanced whatever, you'd go nuts and broke," said Alex P. of Palo Alto, California.

Still the average home is full of potential baby danger zones, and the use of some child-safety devices is a necessity. None of us want to see our children hurt, especially in a way we could have easily prevented by screwing a tiny plastic lock onto the knife drawer. But like everything else, childproofing can be taken too far. One child-safety expert suggests removing all lamps from your home because a toddler can pull them down; I say, let there be light. However, I am not a child-safety expert (do not read this book and then blame me if your kid takes a dive into the toilet).

In researching this book, I spoke to numerous guys who *pshaw* nearly all manner of safety lock. But I also heard from several dads who look upon childproofing as a very real opportunity to impose a little control over the chaos that has reigned since their transition into parenthood. And there are also those men who revel in any chance to use a screwdriver. It's common to hear that a home can never be too safe; but I can imagine at least one instance in which "too safe" could cross the line to "dangerous": You're supposed to keep your fire extinguisher away from kids, but do you really want to store it behind a cabinet door with a childproof lock that takes two hands and up to thirty seconds to open? The defense rests.

CHAPTER 13

Fashion Faux Pa

You can tell a lot about a man from the clothes he wears: a Kool-Aid Man T-shirt advertises his ironic, yet hackneyed sense of humor; patched elbows on his sports coat telegraph the fact that he considers himself an intellectual; a backward baseball cap means there's somebody younger he's trying to impress; sweatpants in public means he's either on the way to the gym or lonely. Today, what a man wears may also be able to tell you whether he's a parent—especially if he's wearing a baby.

THE UNITED COLORS OF FATHERHOOD:
Your Style Meets Daddy Style

> "Playing in the sandbox and sliding down the slide is a bit hard on the dry cleaning."   —Eric S., Atlanta, GA

Regardless of your fashion sense, fatherhood may dictate a new look for you—mostly involving clothing with more stains and wet spots. This can be especially hard on men who have historically prided themselves on their trendy appearance.

"I have a lot of nice clothes that serve no purpose now except taking up space in my closet," said one Chicago dad. "I'm afraid to wear a $50 shirt while I'm holding my son. I have no place to wear them anymore anyway."

If you happen to be one of those guys who regularly uses pomade and doesn't shun pants with a sheen to them (the ones we were calling "metrosexuals" during that word's blessedly short run as part of the popular lexicon), you will find that the rigors of parenthood make it harder for you to stay fashionable. Due to a lack of time, you'll have to abbreviate your daily skin care regimen (especially when all your tea-tree-oil-containing products are locked away behind some kind of complicated safety mechanism). And baby commitments will cost you many valuable shopping opportunities. Perhaps worst of all, you will also need to accept the fact that you will always be upstaged by the baby.

But it's not just the denizens of Armani Exchange who need to adjust; rugged, flannel-clad men will one day find themselves peeling covertly planted Hello Kitty stickers from their puffy vests. At some point, you will give up trying to stay clean. When you're with a little kid, having orange cheese-dust handprints on your shirt doesn't convey the same "hygiene-schmygiene" message it does when you're single. Stains that are obviously baby-based tell the world that you are not only a father, but that you are a big enough part of your child's life to have his partially chewed lunch running down your back. Better yet if the mess is dried or caked on: You're too busy parenting to get it cleaned.

THE BJÖRN IDENTITY: Kangaroo Dad

The only thing that screams paternal involvement more than wearing your baby's stains is wearing your baby. Today's dad is not fully equipped without a Baby Björn or a Snugli or some other kind of body-mounted infant carrier. And why wouldn't you want one? They put the stress on your shoulders rather than on your arms, which tire out faster; they free up your hands to do other things, like hold open an unfolded newspaper or dip into a bag of goldfish crackers; they're a lot easier to get through revolving doors than strollers; they score you some blue-ribbon bonding time with the baby while finally allowing you the cathartic opportunity to (sort of) replicate your wife's experience of lugging around the baby during the pregnancy. And you won't even realize how much damage they're doing to your back until you take them off. (Whenever people talk about the cost of raising a child, they never factor in the chiropractor bills.)

You can go chest-bound, which allows for easy head-kissing access and no fear of losing sight of the child, but makes it decidedly more difficult to do a crossword puzzle; or you can choose a back-pack carrier, which provides what should be a far more familiar sensation and allows for good enough range of motion to score high on a Galaxian machine, but which, lacking rearview mirrors, leaves you completely in the dark as to whether or not your child is trying to yank the tails of nearby squirrels or suck on the brim of a passer-by's hat.

There is also the sling, an all-cloth contraption that allows for sidesaddle carrying. There are women who swear by the sling, but from both my own experience, as well as anecdotal evidence from other dads, I can tell you it doesn't often elicit the same euphoric response from men. Appearing as nothing more than a blanket knotted into a circle, the sling envelops your infant into a supposedly womb-like snugness. But once it's slung over your head, the kid is just hanging there—no belts, no straps—and if you're prone to even the slightest bit of paranoia, you can easily spend your entire sling-wearing time afraid to bend forward even an inch without dumping your passenger onto the floor. Very long instruction booklets and accompanying videos will tell you that the sling can be worn in about five hundred different ways, but none so straightforward as slipping your arms through the shoulder straps of a standard carrier. The sling certainly has its female fans, though, so perhaps there's a physiological component to male deficiency in its use: We have no hips.

No matter what carrier style you choose, though, the importance of wearing your baby as an accessory cannot be stressed enough. To avoid any strangers' unwarranted assumptions of laziness, the proud father shuns being seen walking empty-handed while his wife pushes the stroller. It wouldn't matter if the guy was steering through the mall for hours before his wife graciously offered to give him a break and take over for a while; the first person to see her at the helm while he's unencumbered can still react with a "typical guy" huff.

Until your kid's too big, a baby carrier can eliminate any chance of such a scenario.

THE WHEEL MAN

Your stroller says as much about your personal sense of style as your wardrobe. It reveals aspects of your character in the same way your car does, and the baby transport will often match its adult counterpart: Hummer-sized Gracos roll unfolded from the backs of Ford Expeditions; titanium Maclarens are pulled in their compacted states from the trunks of Priuses. You may also feel somewhat constrained in your choice by your geopolitical landscape. Roll a hulking Jeep Wagoneer stroller down the streets of Manhattan and you'll be greeted with xenophobic stares from all the Bugaboo pushers. But this is not just urban elitism; it goes both ways. Take a Stokke Xplory with you while visiting relatives out in SUV country and you'll have incredulous neighbors asking you where the baby's weather-shield and overhead toy rack are.

> "The wheels on our stroller suck; you can't even push the thing very far. But living in the suburbs, our biggest practical concern was finding one that would fold in and out of the trunk of the car easily. For friends who live in the city, that's not even an issue; all they're concerned about is not losing the kid while they bounce over the uneven pavement."
>
> —Stuart Z., Baltimore, MD

One danger if you happen to live in a community that is particularly susceptible to peer pressure: Recovering your kid's wheels from any public stroller-parking area turns into a game of Where's Waldo? when all the strollers are the same make. You may have to take the precautionary step of giving your kid's ride a little something extra to make it stand out from the crowd—just like people who tie a brightly colored ribbon to their plain black suitcases for the baggage carousel at the airport. Of course, having something as uncool as a pair of Teletubbies pennants flapping from the handles completely negates the purpose of buying the "in" stroller to begin with.

As a man, you also now have to consider whether or not the stroller you're pushing is too "girlie." In an effort to get men excited about baby gear, manufacturers have decided to milk the male obsession with cars and trucks by shooting up baby carriages with steroids. While marketers might have once expected a father's part in the purchasing decision minimal, they are now counting on us to take over the hunt. All the sales-speak about strollers today is rife with automobile terminology. When wheel size, shock absorbers, aerodynamics, and racing stripes are part of the equation, what red-blooded American male can stand by and let his wife make that kind of call? You need to step in and say: "Honey, we're getting the Sports Utility Ironman stroller—I don't care if it won't fit through our doorway." Even as a guy who thinks of my Saturn as the coolest car I've ever owned, I have to admit, it's easy to become entranced by baby buggies that are just so damn attractive. Should you sense this happening, you must take a step back and ask yourself, "How often will I really take the stroller off-roading?"

THE BAG MAN

When you have a child, leaving your house becomes an event unto itself. The number of items you need to tote along keeps rising, and preparing to go out for a short afternoon stroll begins to look like you're packing for a year abroad. When you were a baby, you were probably carried out with nothing more than a spare diaper, a bottle, and possibly some saltines in case you got a rumbly tummy. Today, the checklist just keeps getting longer: You need diapers, wipes, bibs, pacifiers, teething rings, a few changes of clothes, diaper rash cream, medicines, droppers, Band-Aids, a bottle of formula and a bottle of water (or a drink box for toddlers), several books, a selection of toys large enough to cover any form of stimulation (mental, oral, tactile), at least four Baggies loaded with various snack choices, ad infinitum. The idea behind the overpacking is that you, as a good parent, need to be prepared not only for any kind of emergency, but also for the proper appeasement of whatever mood should strike your baby while you are out. Why else would you hear playground conversations like this:

TODDLER: Hungry.
MOTHER: Cracker?
TODDLER: No.
MOTHER: Carrot stick?
TODDLER: Uh-uh.
MOTHER: Raisins?
TODDLER: Don't like.
MOTHER: Apple slice?
TODDLER: No.
MOTHER: Cookie?
TODDLER: Want breadstick.
MOTHER: Okay, sweetie, let's head back home.

So the question arises: How are you going to carry all this crap? If you have any crazy ideas about throwing everything into a backpack, wipe those thoughts from your mind immediately. In an uncategorized jumble, milk will leak onto dry diapers, crayons will leave marks on library books, dried fruit bits will gum up the joints of posable dolls: No, you need different pockets for everything—pockets with lining. This is the governing principle behind the diaper bag.

If you're a man willing to tote around the over-the-shoulder pocketbook-style bag your wife bought, more power to you. But you no longer need to: An increasing number of companies are offering "dad bags." And there are some nice looking ones out there. The hippest models come in messenger-bag style, sometimes constructed of preweathered leather, and from the outside, give no hint that they contain rubber nipples. The manliest of the dad bags are rugged, weatherproof, flap-happy backpacks—because nothing says "virility" like superfluous pockets. They come in testosterone friendly colors like navy, gray, khaki, and camouflage (so you and your baby can sneak up on deer together), and load you down with more straps and pull-cords than the average skydiver. They will make you appear as if you are on your way to scale K2 rather than replenish your supply of sippy-cup lids.

Does your family really need to spend money on a second bag just so you won't have to carry something remotely purse-like in public? On the other hand, shouldn't we be heartened by the fact that these baby-goods companies are taking the rare step of considering fathers part of their customer base and beginning to design products specifically for them? But, then again, isn't the presumed need for a separate "male" diaper bag based entirely on gender stereotypes? And when it comes right down to it, shouldn't we admit that guys just like cool stuff? These are all good questions.

CHAPTER 14

Sympathy for the Devil: Children's Television

"I need to remind my son sometimes, 'That only works in cartoons. Don't try that on your sister.'"

—Christopher W., Richmond, VA

TV: They're the two most controversial letters in parenting. We all know that letting your toddler sit in front of the set for dawn-to-dusk viewing of the Cartoon Network is not the most responsible parenting behavior. Banning television from your household is a legitimate choice, and one considered by many to be a more respectable course of action. If you're a true believer in a strict "no TV" policy, it's easy to feel a bit superior to the overly lax parents, as well as *anyone* who admits to occupying their kids with the animated hijinks of talking, often pantsless animals. However, I believe there are not as many true believers as the true believers believe there to be.

THE HIGH-DEFINITION SKELETON IN THE CLOSET

Meet almost any other parents for the first time and mention television; they're likely to answer with something like, "Oh, our child doesn't really watch it." A few weeks into a friendship, that statement will evolve to: "We let him see a video every now and then, but that's it." Get to know the couple well enough and finally you'll hear: "Thank God for Nickelodeon or I'd never get anything done!" Indeed, with very few exceptions, the men I interviewed for this book began their answers to questions about kids watching TV with a disclaimer ("Well, I hate to admit it, but . . ." or "I know it's not really the best thing, but . . ." or "I'm embarrassed to say it, but . . .").

Why all the hedging? Why is everyone so afraid to just come out and say that they occasionally need to *do something,* and that achieving that goal may mean providing their children with the distraction of a cheerily educational television program? It's because in today's culture, it often seems there is no greater sin than exposing your child to SpongeBob SquarePants. The No-TV folks have science on their side: The American Academy of Pediatrics sets guidelines that allow for no more than one to two hours of television a day for children ages three and up, and for younger kids: zip, zero, zilch, nada—no moving images on any kind of screen. As the AAP writes, "The first 2 years of life are especially important in the growth and development of your child's brain. During this time, children need good, positive interaction with other children and adults."

Well put. No one can refute that. But using it as a rationale for a total television ban implies that parents should be providing stimulation for their baby during every waking hour. And that just feeds into the absolutist mentality that is giving today's parents ulcers and anxiety disorders. If you spend adequate time entertaining, cuddling, and talking to your eighteen-month-old, you should be able to pop in a *Baby Einstein* DVD while you make dinner and not worry that doing so might cause irrevocable damage to your child's developing brain.

I'm not condoning couch-potatoism for our nation's youth; far from it. Ninety-eight percent of what's on TV is bad for kids (probably a good 92 percent is bad for *anybody*). The AAP rightly rails against TV's rampant violence, increasingly scatological language, and glorification of drug and alcohol use—but you don't run into much of that on *Miffy and Friends*. And even among children's programming, there's a mighty big difference between *Sesame Street* and the latest hit Japanese import about exploding robots.

Just as kids learn bad things from television, like skateboarding and kissing, they can learn good things, too, like table manners and how many sides a hexagon has (FYI: six). My four-year-old can spout off about as much Spanish as most adults who try to recall the full year of language they took when they were high school freshmen; this is not because I drilled Bryn with Berlitz lessons in her high chair, but because of *Dora the Explorer*. There have been studies showing that kids who watch high-quality educational programming score better on reading and math tests than children who are confined to TV-free households. The AAP mentions those findings in its guidelines.

So let's just admit that our kids watch TV—then we can move on and discuss it.

THE OPIATE OF THE MASSES: The Zombification Effect

When dealing with preschoolers and TV, sex and violence shouldn't be your biggest concern. I will give you enough credit to assume you're not treating your toddlers to viewings of *The Sopranos* or *Hannity & Colmes*. But even assuming your child's TV time is limited solely to Muppetational fare, you need to beware of television's more insidious effects.

Regardless of subject matter, TV has a strangely hypnotic, somewhat addictive quality. I'm sure you're familiar with it. It's what kept you Velcroed to your sofa cushion staring at *Veronica's Closet* long after *Seinfeld* was over. It's what enables you to spend an hour viewing a program and then answer the question "What are you watching?" with "Nothing."

Children are, if anything, more susceptible to this trance-inducing power than adults. In my research for this book, I saw a good deal of paternal concern, even on the part of dads with decidedly lax TV policies, about the fact they could sometimes not break their child's gaze from the set without hitting the power button. Even though Bryn's television diet consists almost entirely of respectable educational programming along the lines of *Sesame Street* and *Blue's Clues,* my wife and I grew concerned when she started coming home from day care, throwing down her jacket, and saying, "Where's the 'mote?"

Rather than put our TV up for auction, we implemented some rules around viewing. They weren't harsh restrictions; we just didn't want Bryn to start thinking that her favorite episode of *Dora* was always just there for her to watch whenever she felt like it (although, thanks to TiVo, it actually is—*shhhh!*). So we set time limits on viewing. Surprising the hell out of both of us, Bryn accepted this rather graciously. In only a few days, when we clicked the set on, she started saying, unprompted, "Just one show, then TV off."

Many other men have put similar rules into effect in their own homes, and just like I do, they often let those rules stretch a bit when they need some extra time to scrub a floor, answer overdue e-mails, or write a book. Thankfully, with a toddler's poor concept of time, you can pull this off and still stick to a "one show only" rule by popping in the full-length *Many Adventures of Winnie the Pooh* rather than one twenty-two-minute episode of *Thomas & Friends.* As long as your kid isn't cuddling DVDs in bed, the way other children would a plush teddy bear, you're probably okay.

IT'S AN AD, AD, AD, AD WORLD:
The Insidious Evil of Commercials

The other big concern most guys have regarding TV is fear of their kids becoming mind-slaves of the advertising machine. Most of us don't mind our toddlers being innocently engaged by hand puppets explaining the difference between happy and sad, but we're not naive enough to think that the lesson won't be followed up by the appearance of a neurotic leprechaun trying to convince our kids that marshmallows are an important part of a nutritionally balanced breakfast.

Many of today's dads come from the first generation of kids to be entertained by shows that were based on toys, rather than the other way around. We were among the first guinea pigs to experience direct-to-children advertising after government deregulation. We know the power of a good commercial—and if there's any doubt as to how deeply these things embed themselves into our collective subconscious, ask yourself why you still know that Weebles wobble, but they don't fall down; that Super Golden Crisp has the crunch with punch; or that the kid who played Connect Four had a pretty sneaky sis.

At least there was always PBS for commercial-free fare, though sadly that's changed, too. I was distressed to see that recent episodes of *Sesame Street* have been sponsored not just by the Helena Rubinstein Foundation, but by the golden arches as well. At least the marketing messages appear only in between shows, and the episodes themselves, just like the programs on Nickelodeon and the Disney Channel, are uninterrupted by calls for a child's initiation into the world of trans fats. And Noggin (Nick's sister station for under-fives) doesn't push products at all: It's guilty only of self-promotion. So safeguarding your child from ads is a bit easier than it used to be— as long as you have cable, which is ironic, because a lot of parents who don't subscribe to cable say they do it to protect their kids.

We should also be thankful for the introduction of digital video recorders (DVRs) like TiVo machines or the consoles offered by many cable companies. Their fast-forwarding capabilities can save us all, adult and child alike, from ad oppression. Not to mention that in allowing you to record a show and watch it whenever it suits your schedule, a DVR really is a parent's best friend: It lets you keep Big Bird on deck for whenever you might need him, and it gives you the ability to enjoy a TV-14-rated program after your child has gone to sleep. Of course, the DVR's innovations have become the bane of the advertising industry and have caused companies to seek out new methods of slipping their brand names into your subconscious, like product placement. It won't be long, I'm sure, before product placement weasels its way into "educational" children's programming ("Thomas the Tank Engine, we have an emergency mission for you! Sir Topham Hat needs you to haul these bottles of brisk, refreshing Sierra Mist to all the thirsty children at the seashore"), just the way it has insinuated itself into grown-up television shows, movies, and even books. And if the long-standing threat of having banner ads run across your screen while you fast-forward with your DVR should come to pass, such advertisements are unlikely to have the same captivating effect on kids—especially preliterate ones—as full-blown 30-second minimovies starring their favorite toys.

MASTERS OF OUR DOMAIN: Watching with Your Child

So are we being responsible parents when it comes to our children's television viewing? Let's measure ourselves up to the AAP guidelines:

- "Set limits"—check (except for that whole "nothing at all before age 2" part).
- "Help your child resist commercials"—check.
- "Watch TV with your child"—done and done! Now this is one area of parenting where I have to say the dads definitely outclass the moms. Not that a woman can't reinforce the positive lessons of a program, explain the difference between fantasy and reality, or demystify any parts that might be confusing or scary; but when it comes to watching TV with their kids, men are truly in their element.

When Bryn is scribbling away in some *Dora the Explorer* coloring book and asks her mother to join her by handing off a crayon and saying, "Here, Mommy, you do Benny," it still never ceases to amaze me that my wife can stare at the page for a few moments and then start coloring in the squirrel, eliciting shrieks of protest from our daughter. At least fifty some-odd episodes of *Dora* have played in front of my wife—many repeated several times—and she still doesn't know that Benny is the bull. Tico is the squirrel! I mean, come on!

Somehow, my wife has the ability to block out whatever is happening on the TV, to put up a personal firewall that encrypts the exploits of animated woodland creatures into harmless white noise. I, on the other hand, can sing any song from the *Dora* soundtrack and can probably provide you with a scene-by-scene synopsis of any episode. This is not by choice; often, I'm performing some other activity while the show is running—reading a newspaper, sewing a hole in Bryn's jacket, even carrying on a conversation—but at the same time, I'm still absorbing the fact that Dora's train friend, Azul, might not win the race because Swiper the Fox just tossed several portions of the track into the rain forest.

I hate to make sweeping generalizations, but I'm pulling out the broom for this one: Men are more susceptible to television than women.

"I watched *Arthur* this morning," admitted Stuart Z. from Baltimore. "I don't know why. My son had it on, and it's like I was hardwired to pay attention. Maybe it's sad to say, but I find the show mildly interesting. I know it's not groundbreaking television, but at least I know I'm watching something better than anything with Jim Belushi."

Through some kind of biological deficiency, we are unable to put up the same kind of deflector shields that women use to protect themselves from pop-culture trivia. From one guy after another, I heard about wives who couldn't sort out the casts of their children's favorite shows, who couldn't recall the lyrics to theme songs, who were unable to recognize a new episode from a rerun.

It would appear to be that when a television is on anywhere in the room, a man is paying attention to it, even if not on a conscious level ("I'm not even a big baseball fan," one dad revealed to me, "but if there's a game playing in the corner of a restaurant, even though I'm fully engaged in a conversation with my wife, some percentage of my brain is taking in what's happening on that set"). This is an automatic and uncontrollable function of the male psyche. And the information sticks. I will admit, though, that occasionally it's not subliminal; you may at some point find yourselves actually caring to see what will happen on a kids' show. This is when your wife will make fun of you.

> "One time I was upstairs working on my computer. My wife and daughter weren't home at the time. I went down to grab a drink and the TV was on; we were taping a *Sesame Street* for my daughter to watch later. I noticed it was one I hadn't seen yet: Telly had found a baby duck and wanted to keep it as a pet, but everyone was telling him how the duckling had to get back to its mother. There I was sitting on the sofa watching *Sesame Street* all by myself. I was really curious to see what was going to happen to the duck."   —Brett C., Cleveland Heights, OH

The downside to all of this is obvious: less room in the brain for useful information, like tax code or the location of your car keys. There is a benefit, though, to knowing that Murray is the Wiggle in the red shirt or that Blue and her friends can "skidoo" into storybooks. Rather than just being mind-numbing fluff, the songs and catchphrases of kids' shows can instead form the foundation of a common language between you and your child. Mention Captain Feathersword or Spud the Scarecrow to your preschooler and you can elicit the same kind of respect and appreciation you get from the citizens of a foreign country when they realize you put in the effort to learn some of their native language before vacationing on their turf.

But the benefits of your mind being engulfed by the minutiae of children's programming don't stop there: This same trivia will also be the basis of a shared mythology between you and other dads, much in the same way that almost any two men in the country can meet for the first time and carry on a conversation made up entirely of *Simpsons* references. Even if there's not a single other thing in common between you and another man, if you notice that both your child and his have *Blue's Clues* backpacks, you know you can pleasantly kill the afternoon by asking, "So, who do you think is the better host, Steve or Joe?"

FIVE THINGS GROWN-UP MEN SHOULD KNOW
ABOUT CHILDREN'S TELEVISION

1. **Elmo will redeem himself to you.** After the introduction of the shrill first-person-phobic Muppet in 1984, he became the instant object of hatred for anyone who had been a viewer of *Sesame Street* in its earlier days. We lived through the Tickle-Me craze thinking of the hairy little red guy as The Monster That Ruined *Sesame Street.* As a parent, though, you will come to see Elmo in a different light. You will not only come to appreciate how much your child adores him—and she will—but there's a very good chance you will find yourself becoming somewhat endeared of the squeaky-voiced freak. He's really quite charismatic. If any new *Sesame* character will ignite your fury, it's Baby Bear.

2. **Barney is watchable.** Sure he's goofy, overly saccharine, and has a freakishly large jaw even for a dinosaur, but that doesn't mean you can't get something out of watching his show. Viewed with an adult sense of humor, *Barney & Friends* works amazingly well as a spoof of musical theater. The dialogue is so corny, the musical numbers so forced, and the emoting by Barney's human children cohorts so farcically over-the-top, that it can be hilarious. So if your child ends up a fan of the show, that might not be as bad a thing as you think. Your kid might just wonder why you're laughing uproariously at BJ's song about feeling lonely.

3. **The rhythm is gonna get you.** The theme songs to a lot of today's big kids' shows are eerily catchy. But if you catch yourself bopping along, fear not. One dad told me about a time he was walking down the street singing the *Elmo's World* theme when he walked past another man in a business suit. The other guy joined in with him.

4. **If it's British, don't expect to understand it.** The Teletubbies were weird enough: They spoke their own gibberish language; they worshipped some kind of giant infant-headed sun; and their "adventures" didn't seem to consist of much more than frolicking in a field and taking breaks to watch strange interstitials on one another's bellies. *Boohbah* is even worse. I defy anyone to explain *Boohbah*. It appears to be about seven different colored fuzzy globules that live in a flying plastic ball and do nothing but bounce around like Oompa-Loompas on crack for the whole show. What you're supposed to learn from this is beyond me.

5. **You must be prepared for the possibility of being stumped by *Blue's Clues*.** While Joe (or Steve) sits in his Thinking Chair to contemplate the possible meaning of the day's clues, if you find yourself shouting out answers as if you were watching *Jeopardy!* by yourself, you wouldn't be the first guy to do so. The day you get the solution wrong, though—in front of your child—will precipitate a serious ego check.

ADULT ENTERTAINMENT: Your Child, Homer, and You

Children assume anything animated is meant for them. This creates a dilemma for millions of men across the nation. As one father I spoke to put it, "I sometimes worry that the boy might see a little too much of a certain yellow family."

Considered the pinnacle of entertainment by so many American men, *The Simpsons* is one guilty pleasure we just can't let go of. Station programmers taunt us by running syndicated reruns sixteen times a day. You might have the early seasons on DVD. And if you happen to own any toys as an adult, there's a decent chance they're Simpsons collectibles. How can you not share such an important part of your life with your child?

You know the show is not meant for kids, but you figure, "The adult humor is going to go right over their heads; what's the harm?" Then you watch Nelson pounding on Milhouse and you cringe a little bit; then you see Homer wrap his hands around Bart's throat and you quickly try to distract your kid ("Hey, look over in the corner—is that Santa?"); then the *Itchy & Scratchy* theme starts up and in microseconds you jump in front of the television to block your child's view of a cat being disemboweled and fed its own entrails.

There are legitimate lessons to be gleaned from *The Simpsons*—about family loyalty, self-discipline, tolerance—but, unfortunately, they're buried under deep mounds of satire and require a whole lot of explaining to get through to a three-year-old. If you're a devotee, and you really want to give it a shot, pray that your child identifies with Lisa.

Frankly, *SpongeBob SquarePants* can seem equally inappropriate at times. Though Nickelodeon markets the sartorially challenged aquatic lifeform right alongside Blue and Dora—there are SpongeBob strollers and footie pajamas—there is a huge age gap between the target audiences of these shows that many parents are overlooking. Don't get me wrong, SpongeBob can be downright hilarious, but the humor is usually either too crude (underwear jokes and exploding eyeballs) or too sophisticated (allusions to Quint from *Jaws* or gags about union-busting) for someone still learning their ABCs. I suspect that, like *The Simpsons,* this is a cartoon fathers don't mind watching with their kids because they dig it so much themselves.

But bad behavior can be found all over kids' TV, even in "good" shows that teach lessons by having their protagonists act badly. The trains of *Thomas & Friends* constantly engage in jealous name-calling; Caillou whines about everything; Franklin the turtle lies and refuses to share. Despite the fact that these characters are always chastened and supposedly learn the error of their ways in the end,

MEN ON FILM

Perhaps you remember this JCPenney commercial from a few years back (several of the guys I interviewed brought it up almost immediately when I asked for their thoughts on television depictions of fatherhood): Unruly children have staged a hostile takeover of their family kitchen. The place is a complete wreck, with food spilled everywhere, and the baby in the high chair is throwing things. A befuddled, half-dressed father surveys the scene with a look of panic on his face. "Where is your mother?" he blurts out. Mom, it turns out, has abandoned her family to run off to JCPenney's big One Day Sale.

For our current purposes, we'll ignore how offensive this ad is to women and just focus on the male perspective. The reason this commercial stuck in the memories—and the craws—of so many guys is that it was a quintessential example of the incompetent dad stereotype that has persisted in the media since the invention of the kinetoscope. From *Mr. Mom* to *Daddy Day Care,* Hollywood has envisioned nothing funnier than a man trying to care for a child. Look at *Three Men and a Baby;* the title says it all—you wouldn't have to know anything else about the film to guess that somewhere along the course of those ninety minutes at least one man will get peed on and another will be flummoxed by the workings of a baby bottle. *Full House* stretched this concept into about nineteen seasons. In the JCPenney commercial, we saw the caricature at its most farcical: Here is a guy with an undetermined number of kids (you can't tell in all the clutter; perhaps he's not even sure) and the moment there's no woman in the room, he crumbles like a cookie in the mouth of a Muppet.

Sure, there *are* men like this. But if you went solely based on the world of entertainment, you'd think we were all dundering oafs in the presence of children. Sitcoms are the worst offenders; with very few exceptions, the fathers are clueless. And those who are not have historically overcompensated with a near-unshakable calm and a never-ending supply of aphorisms on tap (Cliff Huxtable, Steven Keaton, Mike Brady). Perhaps ironically, *Sex and the City* gave us one of recent history's best TV dads in the character of Steve Brady (played by David Eigenberg). He was an amiably acerbic basketball-playing bartender, and remained so even as he unabashedly doted on his baby son and pulled in at least a good 50 percent of the child-care duties. But for every Steve, there are ten Ray Barones, whose kids—on the rare occasions that they were seen—only served as foils to addle their hapless father.

Even in the world of television advertising, there is hope: During the course of writing this book, I happened to see a Cheerios spot that contained a completely realistic, totally inoffensive depiction of a man with a child. The father sits on his sofa, reading a newspaper and eating a bowl of cereal at the same time, all with baby balanced on his knee. As the tot snacks on Cheerios from a pile of oat circles before him, he leans over and steals one from dad's bowl. The father responds with, "Hey, eat your own." Some might say this guy is not paying enough attention to the kid, that he's not fully engaged in his son's feeding, that his flippant attitude means he's not taking fatherhood seriously enough. I say he's the guy we should all strive to be.

their epiphanies can be as difficult to spell out for a preschooler as Bart's realization that it was wrong for him to cut the head off the statue in the Springfield town square.

In the end, none of it is as difficult as trying to watch the evening news with your kid in the room. Don't even attempt that one.

"My son loves Elmo and Jon Stewart. Whenever he hears the *Daily Show* theme, he just perks right up."

—Ed C., Dunwoody, GA

CHAPTER 15

Song Sung Blues

Most of us probably don't remember our parents complaining about our taste in music until we were teenagers. But everywhere I look today, I see parents' nostrils flaring at the mere mention of children's music. The ease with which the cloyingly trite melodies of most kids' songs can get trapped in adult heads fuels a fear and hatred of these classic ditties.

Many dads I interviewed declared their intention to avoid the genre all together. And if you've got the same goal in mind, here's some good news: While exposing your child to your grown-up television shows is a cardinal sin, forcing him to listen to your grown-up music is not only acceptable but often lauded. When you let a child watch an adult TV program, you're poisoning his mind; when you let him listen to adult music, you're broadening his horizons. So no worries if you've already got the primary-colored plastic CD player you bought for your baby loaded with Hoobastank.

However, while you are free to expose your child to more sophisticated riffs than those of Raffi, you must realize that there's no escaping the classics. You will discover that, despite your best efforts to introduce your child to eclectic artists and genres, the opening notes of "This Old Man" will still get him up and moving as fast as would a triple espresso.

There's a reason why "Row Row Row Your Boat" is a standard. It's short, repetitive, and catchy; everything kids love. While preschoolers may have a blast shimmying to Louis Prima's growly "Jump Jive an' Wail," they're not going to learn the lyrics. And when it comes to singing, kids want songs they can really wrap their developing minds around, a tune they can get to know backward and forward. That's a contest where it's hard to beat "Mary Had a Little Lamb" or "Old MacDonald."

These songs just ain't going away, guys. So it's better to learn to make peace with the classic kids' tunes rather than sit and fume every time your child asks you for another rendition of "She'll Be Coming 'Round the Mountain." However, your kid's musical diet doesn't need to be 100 percent campfire sing-along. Not only can "grown-up" songs find their way onto your child's playlist, but a new crop of more complex kids' tunes may appeal to your adult ear as well.

ROCK YOUR BABY: Kid-Friendly Grown-up Music

"I don't have a single tape or CD of kids' music—I simply refuse. My daughter gets plenty of it from swim class, gymnastics, and actual music class. She is an Eminem fan. She hears everything from hip-hop to rock to classical to opera to bluegrass to blues. No jazz, though—I can't stand jazz."

—Herb S., San Francisco, CA

As parents, we're constantly told to expose our children to music, so wouldn't it be nice to have the songs we play for them be ones we like as well? "If the parents can't dig the songs, then the child's experience of discovering music is a very different one from a situation in which the kid and the parents are grooving on it together," says Pete Cenedella, a New York dad who fronts a rock band, American Ambulance. "I grew up listening to the Beatles and rediscovered how beautiful their music is by playing it for my girl."

"Right now, my baby listens to whatever I'm listening to," said Las Vegas dad Chris F. "I figure there's eventually going to be a time that she starts asking to hear specific kids' songs, like 'Itsy Bitsy Spider' or whatever. I see no reason to rush there."

When it comes to grown-up music, not all songs are created equal in the eyes of children. While you can never guess what a kid might or might not like, you can make an educated guess that your toddler won't be humming along with Slipknot. I've heard several guys swear by the kid appeal of Dixieland, bluegrass, and reggae (Bob Marley's *Legend* disc was one of Bryn's early faves; I heard multiple testimonials for the *O Brother, Where Art Thou?* soundtrack). The key appears to be finding melodic songs with a bouncy beat; oft-repeated, singable choruses don't hurt either.

Your tot might happily bounce around the living room to James Brown or Barenaked Ladies, but dancing isn't the only reason you play music; it's also a centuries-old sleep aid. When you're looking to bring the mood down, don't resign yourself to recordings of Brahms plinked out on toy piano. Why not Tony Bennett or Norah Jones? "My favorite lullaby album of all is definitely Willie Nelson's *Stardust,*" said Cenedella. "Perfect for kids, but made for grown-ups."

CROSSOVER APPEAL: Grown-up–Friendly Kids' Music

We are, of course, not the first generation of parents trying to raise their children on the music of our own favorite artists. In the sixties, when folk was having its heyday, all the groovy dads and moms

---

DIY LULLABY

You can score big points with your child by creating your own songs. And if you're not the most musically gifted person in the world, don't be afraid to rip off the tune of an oldie. Have you ever realized how many kids' songs are sung to the same melody as "Twinkle, Twinkle, Little Star"? Just call it sampling.

There's a little nonsense song that I made up when Bryn was about nine months old (and which, as a friend pointed out to me years later, blatantly stole the tune of the old *Flipper* theme). It has eight rhyming lines about "Brynnie, Queen of the Ocean," and always made her giggle because her name is repeated so frequently within the lyrics. Years later, that little ditty is still a part of her regular bedtime ritual. What I didn't realize until recently was that she'd been studying my wife and me as we sang the song, learning the words so that one day she could sing it along with us. Now she probably appears to the general public as one of the most self-confident four-year-olds in the world as she walks through the park singing about herself.

---

were joining their kids in sing-alongs of "Puff the Magic Dragon" and "If I Had a Hammer"—so much so that the sound of the acoustic lovefest became the standard for new children's music. If a parent didn't want to listen to a chorus of off-key kindergartners belting out "Skip to My Lou," he just put on a record of Pete Seeger covering the song.

This first era of parent-friendly kids' music unfortunately gave seed to the trilly folk takeover of the nineties, when many of the children who grew up thinking "folk is for kids" started making music themselves. During my unfortunate postcollege stint as an employee at a toy store, I regularly ducked into the break room for coffee shots to keep myself from being anesthetized on the work floor by the achingly boring songs that spilled from the loudspeakers. It seemed that every other album was a collection of vaguely melodic whisperings about wishes and rainbows from artists that sounded like Carly Simon mumbling under hypnosis.

Much of the folksy kids' stuff of the sixties and seventies may seem a bit cheesy today, but at least it was *fun* for its listeners. The purveyors of nineties kids' folk apparently forgot that part, since their recordings served the same basic purpose as a white noise machine. The musical equivalent of foam padding, these gossamer-voiced dronings lacked all the essentials of good children's music— no beat, no sing-alongability. In my opinion, the era was the nadir of kids' music. And we're not completely out of it yet: Kenny Loggins's mournful *Return to Pooh Corner* album is still among Amazon.com's top-selling children's CDs more than a *decade* after its release. This aural Novocain can make you long for the exuberant torture of "Ninety-nine Bottles of Beer on the Wall."

Thankfully, the children's music genre has undergone a bit of a renaissance as of late. With kids' albums hitting the upper strata of the mainstream *Billboard* charts, kids' music is a bigger business today than in the past. This could be in part because the songs themselves are just getting better, but I believe it's also a side effect of how much more present parents are in their children's lives. We're not just tossing a record on the turntable and strolling off to smoke a pipe while our toddlers struggle on their own to figure out when to clap during "Bingo." No, we're skipping, stomping, and twirling right along. We're learning the lyrics and leading the kids through the choruses like latter-day Mitch Millers.

Savvy artists have recognized the fact that even if there's a cow driving a car on the CD cover, adults will hear the music, too. Take alt-pop outsiders They Might Be Giants. Their 2004 disc *No!* supplied them with the biggest sales of their twenty-year career; and it also happened to be the first of their albums marketed directly to children. *No!* doesn't sound all too different from the rest of their mostly kid-friendly catalog, so adult fans—myself included—have been more than happy to pop in the CD.

Dan Zanes, late of the grown-up rock group the Del Fuegos, has spent the last several years building his rep as a kiddie superstar by winning over adult fans. Zanes puts his own funkier spin on the folk-for-kids theme, filling in the missing link between the music a lot of today's parents grew up with and the tracks they currently have on their iPods. "We're big Dan Zanes fans in my house," one thirty-something dad said to me, following up with: "Well, at least I'm a fan. I guess I can't really say whether my kid's into him or not."

The songs of Laurie Berkner—whose videos, like Zanes's, have become a staple on the Noggin network—are unmistakably written for kids. They're bouncy and silly, with subject matter like dinosaurs, crazy hats, and bicycling fish; and yet, they're completely inoffensive to the adult ear. Their infectious melodies are likely to get trapped in your head long after you turn off the stereo, but, believe it or not, you may not mind. Berkner has also shown herself to be adept at the grown-up allusion: the song "Doodlebugs," for instance, off her *Whaddaya Think of That?* CD, while ostensibly about some breed of imaginary insect, is a thinly disguised litany of *Seinfeld* references (the Doodlebug named Jerry flies down to Florida to see his parents).

Despite the emergence of these fence-straddling artists, there are still plenty of kids' musicians who make no outward attempts to seduce grown-up listeners and continue to thrive. The Wiggles are probably the prime example—and three of those guys used to be in punk bands! But if "Willaby Wallaby Woo" doesn't appeal to your art-rock sensibility, you can still have a certain amount of respect for the earnestness of the Aussie quartet. In videos, Berkner and Zanes come off pretty cool, whereas the Wiggles wear monochromatic shirts in the vein of the original *Star Trek* cast and dance with a big foam octopus. The Wiggles play it straight to the kids and keep on winning; They're international superstars who routinely sell out arena concerts.

Luckily for you, the children's music scene is much hipper than it has arguably ever been. Dads I spoke to were pleasantly surprised how much they themselves liked the upbeat folk of Justin Roberts, the modern rock of Ralph's World, and the Muppet garage band sound of ScribbleMonster & His Pals (possibly the edgiest kids' band on the scene today). But musical taste is, of course, one of the most subjective things in the world—for both adults and children. I remember being five and wondering why my classmates looked so happy to be singing "I Know an Old Lady Who Swallowed a Fly," a song which, even then, I thought was absolutely wretched.

CHAPTER 16

A Picture *Is* Worth a Thousand Words: Kids' Books

Whether you're a man who takes in a chapter or two of Tom Clancy on the train to work in the morning, or one who'll search a used bookstore for another copy of *Things Fall Apart* after the original paperback you got in high school finally succumbs to its titular destiny—the transition from grown-up books to kids' books can be a frustrating one. Not that board books don't have their upside (you'll never need to search for a bookmark!), but over time, the singsongy writing, the self-consciously silly plots, and the endless repetition can begin to numb your brain.

Sometimes you might even wonder why you bother reading to your baby—especially in the very beginning, when a child's interest in books is all about the pictures and the words themselves don't mean a thing. The more literary-minded among you may begin to fear the loss of any ability to nab the brown chip in Trivial Pursuit, as you feel the part of your mind that normally functions as an archive for literary allusions start to disintegrate into nothing but a cache of rhymes about body parts.

It's important to remember that there *will* come a time when reading to your child can be a pleasure for both of you. Until that happens, you need to find ways to make your seventy-third reading of *Spot Goes to the Farm* bearable.

LITERATURE THROUGH THE AGES: Reading to Infants vs. Reading to Toddlers

In the first few years of life, your baby's relationship with books will go through several different phases. As she grows from captive audience to tyrannical critic, the way in which you read to her will evolve as well.

0 to 6 Months

When you read to your child during this period, it will often be from a four-page cloth book (meaning the text is printed on what appear to be discarded fabric swatches from a textile factory), often with a simple noun title like _Pets_ or _Flowers_. These soft minivolumes help your newborn to become familiarized with the concept, look, and delicious taste of books, which will only enhance her appreciation of them later on. Also, there is zero chance of a paper cut. However, if these infant haiku—which usually appear to be authored by toy companies rather than actual human beings—are the only volumes you share with your child during this time, you're doing yourself a major disservice.

Yes, it's important for your newborn to grow accustomed to the sound of human speech, but since a four-week-old isn't going to react any differently to "Blue. Shoe." than "It was the best of times, it was the worst of times," you've pretty much got license to read to him from just about anything. Use this latency period to plow through whatever seven-hundred-page novel you bought three years ago when everybody was raving about it and then never got around to cracking open.

"I read to my daughter from whatever I'm reading," said Jeff R. of Chicago, "whether it's Philip Roth or _Esquire_."

There's no reason why your chosen reading material even has to have a story. Once you've read a few baby books and gotten the cadence down, you should be able to pick up a take-out menu and read it aloud as if it were Mother Goose.

"My son had a very early interest with lights, so I showed him a lighting fixture catalog," said Eric S. of Atlanta. "Well, he just loved it, looking at all the pictures of light fixtures and comparing them to the ones in our home. That catalog has found a permanent space in his basket of books."

6 to 18 Months

The shift from suckable cloth to stiff laminated cardboard will occur just as your child becomes aware of the fact that the words you speak during story time are somehow related to the reading material. (Note: Despite their dry-erase-board-type finish, your average board book does have an Achilles' heel, namely the uncoated outer edges of the pages, which are not immune to saliva damage.) This is also the age at which you'll want to stop reading David Mamet plays to the baby; you might begin to fear that the infant's first word will start with "F."

A lot of board books are entirely about the pictures; the words are just there as captions. Sometimes the story is so slight, you may want to augment the text just so you don't feel like you're short-changing your baby. A lot of dads pad story time by pointing out every detail of the illustrations ("Oh, look, there's a ball back there in the corner"), and it ends up taking twenty minutes to read something that is technically only seven sentences long.

One method a lot of dads use for keeping both themselves and their babies interested: Sing the book. Pretty much anything written in verse will work for this purpose, but a lot of guys recommend the works of board-book queen Sandra Boynton or any of the bite-size abridged editions of Dr. Seuss. (Why abridged? Wait a year or so until you have to read through all seventy-two pages of the uncut *One Fish, Two Fish, Red Fish, Blue Fish*—then you'll understand.)

However, the biggest potential problem in the first year or two is Board-Book Conditioning, in which your mind comes to expect denouement by page twelve. Whether you're reading a magazine article or a graphic novel, by about the fifth minute or so, your brain is ready to move on to the next story. Even when flipping through a newspaper, you may be unable to work your way through anything longer than a police blotter item or a pie chart. Forget the next Harry Potter.

18 Months to 3 Years

In a sad confluence of events, the books your child wants to hear get exponentially longer at the same time that she develops the desire to manipulate the length of her bedtime ritual. As you find yourself plodding through the florid prose of *The Tale of Benjamin Bunny* one night, you'll long to go back to the days when your kid would be satisfied with the twenty-eight-word total of *Fuzzy Fuzzy Fuzzy!* Fortunately, the more complex plots also stand a chance of being more interesting; the right children's book can draw you into its world the same way the right kids' TV show can. More than one man admitted to me his disappointment when his child didn't choose Daddy's favorite book for that night's bedtime story.

YOU: Okay, bedtime. Tonight we'll read *Where the Wild Things Are.*
CHILD: No. I want *Where Is Ernie?*
YOU: Honey, we read *Where Is Ernie?* last night. Let's do *Wild Things* tonight.

CHILD: I want Ernie.

YOU: No *Wild Things?* You sure? Do you remember it? Max goes to the island with all the big monsters. Don't you like that one?

CHILD: It's okay. I wanna hear Ernie.

YOU: Okay. (Opening *Where Is Ernie?*) Let's see. So one night Ernie put on his wolf suit to make some mischief.

CHILD: That's not how it goes!

For every worthwhile children's book, there are about a hundred bombs. And in the parenting version of Murphy's Law, whichever book you despise the most will be the one your child loves best. In my own home, more than one undesirable piece of kid-lit has gone the way of Jimmy Hoffa. My wife and I can never bring ourselves to actually trash-can a book for which our daughter has displayed any true fondness, and that softheartedness has proved to be our downfall. Even if it's long after she's forgotten about a hidden book's existence, Bryn always eventually digs it up from under the couch or the back of a closet, and the excitement of rediscovery only serves to reignite her interest in reading the offending material . . . over and over and over again.

ABANDONED BY OPRAH: Good Book? Bad Book?

In the interest of your own sanity, you will probably want to have a wide variety of reading options at the ready whenever story time comes around. But with the children's areas of most bookstores now rivaling the Mall of America in terms of size and number of distractions, finding the good stuff can be a challenge. Here are seventeen observations about children's books that may help you in your search. And for any of you who already have small children and may already be feeling the effects of Board-Book Conditioning, I'll keep them all brief.

1. It always pays to take a book for a test-drive before you buy it. If during an in-store read, your child wanders away to stare at cookbook covers, don't waste your money. Even if it won a Caldecott Medal.

2. Steer clear of any book that has the words "Based on the teleplay . . ." on the cover.

3. Many a modern parent may wonder why those old Brothers Grimm tales had to be so terrifying, but remember that back in fifteenth-century Bavaria, a child wandering off into the woods alone really stood a good chance of being devoured by something.

4. If we were to measure the importance of a childhood lesson by its frequency of appearance in kids' books, we would have to believe that the most vital information any baby should learn is which onomatopoeic sound belongs to which farm animal.

5. It's amazing what you won't remember from the books you loved as a kid. I had interviewees who were shocked to see Curious George smoke a pipe or to discover that the Little Engine That Could was hauling jack-knives to all the good little boys and girls on the other side of the mountain.

"Another very problematic book is *The Cat in the Hat Comes Back*. The incessant reiteration of the word 'kill' (from the little cats 'killing' the spots near the end) seems the work of a man who never had to teach a three-year-old boy why 'killing' is bad and why we don't joke about it. He's like the deranged uncle

who gives inappropriate toys to your kids and makes you the
bad guy for taking them away."

—Eric S., University Heights, OH

6. The more acclaimed the illustrator, the more difficult it is to figure out which animal is supposed to be represented by the stylized conglomeration of shapes that is the book's protagonist.

7. Nothing good can come of books with an electronic control panel
   of buttons attached. But they will always be the first ones your
   child heads for in the bookstore.

8. Pop-up books have an approximate shelf-life of five days. After
   that, you should expect to pick up the book and see a bunch of
   cardboard characters rain down to the floor like subscription
   cards from a magazine.

9. If the illustrator's name appears in a font twice the size of the author's, the dialogue will most likely blow.

10. Keep your alphabet books separate from your storybooks. If you
    get stuck reading an ABC book to your child as a bedtime story,
    by the time you get to "N," you'll be praying for your wife to
    sneak into the room and chloroform you.

11. Books with no words might make you think you're getting off
    easy, but they're actually a lot more work. Your kid's not going to
    just let you turn the pages without saying anything. So you'd bet-
    ter be good at improv.

12. Books illustrated with photographs think they're smarter than
    the ones that only have drawings.

13. While on a certain level, you can respect an ABC book that goes
    with more unconventional word choices, like "I is for ibex," that
    appreciation will fade when you have to repeatedly explain to

your toddler what an ibex is ("No, it's not a goat. Goat starts with
'G.' But that wasn't a goat on the 'G' page, either. That was a gnu.
Yes, I know they both look like goats").

14. Stories with potential to become performance art can help make
repeated readings more tolerable.

"I've perfected my dramatic reading of *Good Night, Gorilla* with
character voices and everything. My daughter likes it, but it
also keeps me interested when we're reading the book for the
thousandth time."   —Bill B., Brooklyn, NY

15. You never know exactly what's going to scare the hell out of your
kid. When I was young, I thought the falling flapjacks in *Cloudy
with a Chance of Meatballs* were the coolest thing in the world,
yet they terrified Bryn to the point of syrup-drenched nightmares.

16. Writing children's books has become the hobby du jour for
celebrities: Base your purchase on the merit of the material, not
what the author wore to the Emmys.

17. Dust jackets don't stand a chance.

CHAPTER 17

Dads in Toyland

Does our generation cling to childhood a little bit too tightly? Well, maybe. The case can certainly be made that men today in their twenties, thirties, and even forties have a somewhat irrational attachment to their pasts. Hence, the popularity of VH1's *I Love the 80s,* adult dodgeball leagues, and Atari Classics collections (so we can experience the monochromatic rectangles of *Breakout* on our 160-gigabyte PCs).

Thankfully, parenthood provides us with a perfectly legitimate excuse to start visiting Toys "R" Us again on a regular basis. But before you start out on your newly sanctioned shopping sprees, there are a few things you should be prepared for.

THE RISE OF THE MACHINES: Wishing the Batteries Weren't Included

When you were a kid, your parents hated any toy of yours that made noise. You thought this was just because they were a couple of codgery old killjoys. Well, they didn't have it half as bad as we do now. What did they have to endure? Maybe a car that made engine sounds or the monotonous pinging of a Tiger handheld LCD game? Today, everything is wired.

Toys that never used to be electronic—and never needed to be electronic—are electronic. Somebody thought that despite almost fifty years of children having fun with old-fashioned corn-popper push toys, today's kids would better appreciate one that flashed colored lights and shrieked out tinny synthesizer music (Fisher-Price has kept their original mercifully unmodified). And as it turns out, letter magnets weren't doing enough multitasking by teaching us to spell while holding crayon drawings to the refrigerator; now they speak, too. Sit 'n Spins once did nothing more than get us sickeningly dizzy and dump us on the floor when we lost our grip—today they add to our nausea by blaring out what sounds like the lost demo tapes of C + C Music Factory. When the average toddler can amuse himself for hours with a pot and a wooden spoon, why does every toy marketed to him need to play a techno version of the "Mexican Hat Dance"?

Many of these screaming, wailing, whining toys seem designed with the specific goal of parental breakdowns in mind. How else can you explain the lack of volume control on so many of them? Even the few items that do have some sort of method for controlling the sound level often provide only two settings: "loud" and "oh my God, my ears are bleeding." It's as if toy manufacturing has been taken over by Spinal Tap ("These go to eleven").

> "We have a new least favorite toy: an extremely noisy guitar that turns itself on if you bump it."   —Bill B., Phoenix, AZ

Talking or singing toys are among the most obnoxious of the lot. Countless dolls (or talking houses or talking barns or talking cars) are marketed with the hyped-up claim "Says six different phrases!" pasted across the box, though the fact that some gizmo repeats the same six sentences over and over should not be a selling point. A child's capacity for repetition is nothing less than stunning, but these toys constitute cruel and unusual punishment for parents. And they lead to an uncalled-for bias against the characters they represent. I believe that the reason so many adults are predisposed to hate Elmo is because, having never watched him on *Sesame Street*, they only know the little red guy from one of his many singing doll incarnations. It's like women who hate Batman based solely on the Joel Schumacher movies—completely unfair to the source material.

But fear not, you *can* fight against the tyranny of the electronic toys. First off, don't buy them. I can't recall one single parent I've spoken to who claimed that their child preferred flashing, beeping overstimulation machines to blocks, crayons, or stacking rings. In fact, most lamented the fact that their kids lost interest in the pricier electronic gadgets much faster than with their old-school classic toys. As I write this, I believe we might be seeing the beginning of a backlash, a trend toward the old-fashioning of toys. Lincoln Logs, which, like Tinkertoys, had been "modernized" into plastic, are once again available in their original real wood form. You may have a LeapPad and Dusty the Talking Vacuum Cleaner, but you've probably also got some wooden puzzles from the ubiquitous "Melissa & Doug." Perhaps this comeback for wooden toys is a beneficial side effect of our generation's nostalgia obsession.

Should electronic toys find their way into your home, you still have an exit door available to you, specifically, that little door that covers the battery compartment. If your child is young enough that he doesn't realize the toy is supposed to make noise, he won't expect it to, and won't be disappointed if it is presented to him sans power source.

"If there's a toy that makes noise and gets on our nerves, we never put the batteries in it," said Michael L., a marine stationed in Ewa Beach, Hawaii. "Just let her use her imagination to play with it."

George R., from Austin, Texas, uses another rather ingenious tactic to battle the forces of obnoxious clamor: packing tape. "We have tape over so many speakers in our house," he said. "It works really well. There will still be enough volume that my son can hear the sound while he's playing with the toy, but I can't hear it fifteen feet away."

You have a very limited age window during which you can make use of these strategies. By three, Bryn was very much aware of what batteries were and when they needed to be replaced. I now regret not stealing more Duracells from her playthings while I had the chance.

YOUR CHILDHOOD HAS BEEN MODERNIZED

So many of the dads I spoke to were shocked and dismayed by the many ways in which the beloved playthings of their youth had been altered over the course of time. Prepare yourself for the same. Pretty much any object that provided the younger you with hours of entertainment has undergone a modern makeover. When we see version 2.0 of some of these toys, it's obvious that the changes have been made for safety purposes—but knowing that doesn't stop you from feeling like part of the fun has been sucked away.

The plastic Slinky, for example, may cause fewer lacerations than its metal ancestor but denies a child of that wonderful clinking sound as the limp spring flops down a staircase. And creating a See 'n Say that has a lever rather than a pull cord will certainly prevent accidental strangulation, but I can tell you from experience that impatient toddlers who are not held in check by the slow retraction of the string will just pull the lever over and over in rapid succession, never allowing the warbly voiced narrator to finish explaining which sound the rooster makes.

And then there are the "safety measures" that cause potential problems in their own right. Bryn loved the play telephone she got for her first birthday, but whenever she lifted the receiver to her ear, the cord—which was all of three inches long so that it could never reach around a child's neck—left the plastic base of the phone dangling in the air ready to swing and smack her in the face. We just cut it off completely, leaving our daughter with a cordless phone (which she was happier with anyway because it was more like Mommy and Daddy's).

Some other changes are a bit more perplexing. Fisher-Price Little People are no longer the bald, limbless cylinder beings we used to squeeze into their tiny circular divot bus seats; they now all appear to be rotund escapees from a Botero painting. I can only surmise that self-esteem issues were at the core of that particular transformation, with the current pandemic of childhood obesity leading toy researchers to believe that the portly youth of today would appreciate similarly stocky dolls to play with.

PLAYS NICE WITH OTHERS: Man Meets Toy

Learning to share is an important but sometimes difficult lesson—and I'm talking about you, not your kid ("I am *so* jealous of my kid's toys," said one dad). You'll hear experts say that toys encourage creativity and nourish the imagination, so the parent should let the child direct playtime. Easier said than done, though—especially when you're trying to build a really cool block tower and the kid keeps knocking it down. In such situations, you need to fight the urge to scoop up all the blocks and say, "Just sit and watch what Daddy's making."

Of course, a little demonstration can be useful in some cases. For a solid six weeks or so, every time the Lego bucket was emptied onto our living room floor, my daughter would enlist me in the construction of a bagel store. And my problem with this wasn't even the fact that our building always had to be a bagel store, but that, per her demands, it had to be the exact same bagel store, with the same doors and windows in the same places, and the same little counter inside. After a while I felt the need to say, "No, Bryn, today we're building a pirate ship"—not because of my own lifelong love of all things buccaneer, but because I wanted to show her that Legos could be used in the creation of other structures. You should have seen the cool plank we made, though. It was awesome.

> "We've got this toy with musical blocks that play different tunes. I love it. I'll play with it by myself while my son's playing with something else that I don't find as interesting."
>
> —Lee W., Brooklyn, NY

In the event that your wife should catch you playing with your child's toys at any time when your child is not in the vicinity—the temptation is too great, it *will* happen—here are some ways to escape the situation gracefully:

- "I'm getting this all set up for her so she can play when she wakes up."
- "Would you look at what our son made? Can you believe he's this good?"
- "Have you seen my keys?"
- [Placing the toy in your mouth] "Nope, definitely not a choking hazard. Good."

CONTROLLER ISSUES: The Video-Gaming Father

> "My wife got me an Xbox for Father's Day. I was so happy, but I said to her, 'You realize you just gave me crack, right?'"
>
> —Eric H., Mechanicsville, VA

Among my fondest childhood memories are recollections of the hours I spent gobbling power pellets with my grandfather in the finished basement of his house. But as a senior citizen Pac-Man enthusiast who cherished his Atari 2600, my Pop-Pop was an anomaly for the times. Years later, when my brother and I got our first Nintendo Entertainment System, my father made the appropriate cable connections to the back of our TV set and promptly left us kids to entertain ourselves with the new "toy." Not that my brother and I ever expected anything more from him than tech support—he was an adult. What interest would he have had in a game that seemed to revolve around plumbers kicking turtles? In contrast, today's kids may very well look to Dad to give them a tutorial.

A lot of us who grew up with game controllers in our hands are still spending some part of our spare time moving digitized characters around on our TV screens today—and now we have children of our own. By all logic, this should be a good thing: Here's a common interest shared between father and child, a potential bonding activity. But, *shhhh* . . . I hear no rejoicing in the streets. You see, if there's one thing that the general population can agree is worse for kids than television, it's video games. There's no need for me to go into the reasons why; we've all read countless articles about how PlayStations make our children fat and how *Grand Theft Auto* teaches you to kill hookers.

"I've played *GTA* a bunch of times, and I've taken down a prostitute exactly once—and even then it was only because I'd heard so many newspeople mention that it could be done," said Andrew Bub, father of two and founder of GamerDad.com, a Web site that rates games on a family-friendliness scale. "Still, *Grand Theft Auto* is not for kids. I never play anything violent at all until after my kids are asleep."

Those of you who dread the thought of your Xbox becoming contraband, something that must be hidden from your child like bottles of ouzo or copies of *Maxim*, may wonder how soon it will be before you need to lock up your game consoles. If your baby is a newborn, still generally oblivious to anything other than faces and breasts, do you need to curb your gaming around her? Of course not. It's quite manageable to hold an infant across your arms or over your shoulder and manipulate a game controller at the same time. Just keep the volume down. If the kid's asleep in your arms, it's unlikely that your thumb movements will wake her up. You need to stick to games that are somewhat slower paced, though—role-playing titles work well—because you don't want to attempt any furious button-mashing while keeping your grip on a tiny child.

That kind of gaming freedom lasts for a very short time. As soon as the baby is able to make visual contact with the TV screen, you need to become much more discreet. To kids, computer graphics look like animation, and we know how quickly a baby will become entranced by a cartoon, so your censors may need to kick in even more fiercely than they do with regular television. *Resident Evil* is a nap time game.

Finding games with no frightening imagery can be difficult, but there are some innocuous-yet-fun titles out there that would probably entertain a preverbal spectator as much as—if not more than—an episode of *Boohbah*. If you're the type of player who favors fighting games like *Tekken* or shooters like *Halo,* you may have always looked down upon the safe titles as "kids' games," but you might be surprised by some of them. The *Harvest Moon* series, for instance, has provided the gaming world with consistently engrossing life-on-a-farm simulators. There's nothing about raising virtual sheep and picking virtual tomatoes that should harm your child.

When your child is a bit older and you're ready to introduce him to the world of gaming, it's in the PC realm that you'll find tons of educational software options, from the classic *Reader Rabbit* series to a plethora of licensed-character games that will allow your child to do things like learn shape recognition with the cast of *Dragon Tales.* I was personally blown away by how quickly Bryn mastered the use of a mouse. After only a few minutes of me guiding her tiny hand, she was clicking solo, using the cursor to drag pirate piggies onto their ships in Dora's *Lost City Adventure,* her very first computer game. I was thinking, "Wow, *I* couldn't use a mouse when I was three"—until it occurred to me that they didn't exist then. Suddenly, I understood my grandparents' shock when I was able to program their newfangled VCR for them back in 1982.

It will be a few years yet before Bryn moves into Super Mario land. But just-for-fun games can have something positive to offer, too. "Most people think that a kid is a zombie while he's playing a video game," said Bub, "but that kid's mind is constantly working. He's thinking: How do I get past that door, how do I beat this boss, what's the pattern? It's one of the most mind-stimulating activities out there. In puzzle solving games, it's great for kids to take on the mental challenge and be able to figure out the solution for themselves."

Scientific studies have shown that kids who play video games have better observational skills, faster reaction speed, improved hand-eye coordination, and even heightened self-confidence over

OMERTA: THE SPECIAL CODE OF SILENCE
BETWEEN FATHER AND CHILD

There are bound to be some parent-child activities you enjoy, but which draw disapproving grumbles from your wife. "I slip my kid pieces of candy," said one dad. "I sing my daughter punk songs of questionable taste," said another. Thus, if your wife is prone to hand-holding on the playground slide, you may be reluctant to reveal to her that you have, on occasion, taken the toddler wakeboarding. And certainly, if your spouse rails against the debilitating effects of video games on the minds of children, you might want to be careful that your daughter doesn't identify Pikachu by name in front of her.

It seems that bonding through the illicit is one parenting trait that is uniquely male. The classic television example is Homer and Lisa Simpson developing an unprecedented closeness through the thrill of betting on professional football games. Every Sunday became "Daddy-Daughter Day" and they spent it gambling together happily—until wet blanket Marge discovered them and pointed out the illegality of the activity. Your own personal Daddy-Daughter Day agenda need not be illegal (and if it is, dear God, please stop!), but with prudence, a little in-joke between you and your child can be the first step toward ensuring future hero worship.

those who don't. Steven Johnson's recent book *Everything Bad Is Good for You* details how just about every pop-culture guilty pleasure you can think of has some kind of benefit. Keep a copy handy for the inevitable times that someone chides you for letting your kid near a Game Boy.

As for the video-games-lend-to-the-national-obesity-epidemic argument, well, they do. So limit your child's time with them, just as you should with television. And don't forget about the whole new breed of video games that can make you work up a sweat (and I don't just mean a perspiring forehead when you're facing down the final monster and realize you have only one clip of ammo left). Games that incorporate movement have made a huge gain in popularity over the past few years. Rhythm games, like *Dance Dance Revolution* (in which you, as the title suggests, get up and move your feet) or *Donkey Konga* (in which you need to beat a bongo in time with a song) can give you an honest workout in the course of playing them. They also happen to be some of the most family-friendly titles on the market—as are the games that are played with Sony's EyeToy camera, which puts the player's image onscreen and requires you to swing your arms and jump around. The resulting visuals may be about as technologically stunning as an amusement park karaoke video, but it's undeniably fun and even a toddler will get a kick out of it.

Whether you play video games yourself or not, if your kid begins to show interest in them at some point, lead her toward titles that don't give you nightmares. With the right level of oversight, you shouldn't need to worry about your kindergartner carjacking call girls.

PART VI

THE PURSUIT OF HAPPINESS

After days of hauling around a twenty-pound human being, mealtimes filled with applesauce battles, nights of interrupted sleep, and countless bouts with needling guilt and anxiety, you owe it to yourself to get out there and cut loose a bit. The challenge is learning how to have a good time while wearing filthy clothing, nursing an aching back, and fighting to keep your eyes open. But face that challenge we must, because unhappy parents mean unhappy children, which just leads to parents who are even more miserable.

There are two very different breeds of recreation: The family kind and the grown-up kind. Each is pleasurable in its own distinct ways. But you shouldn't have to choose between dinner at Fuddruckers or a good roll in the hay. It is possible for men with children to engage in leisure activities both with and without their children. But to get the most out of them, you may need to relearn how to have fun.

CHAPTER 18

Stepping Out with My Baby

I'm not going to lie to you: It's a lot more difficult to enjoy any activity on its own merits when you're doing it with your child (e.g., you may have a blast watching your baby's reactions to Mondrian paintings, but you may not be able to pay attention to the art yourself). That doesn't mean you shouldn't try, though. Go ahead—savor a steak while your toddler smears mac-and-cheese on her face or laugh at the misplaced literary allusions in an animated kid-flick. And remember these moments, so that when you finally get to leave the baby at home, you can appreciate an adults-only outing even more.

MEET MR. PIZZA-FACE: Dining Out

When dining out, your list of potential eating establishments is going to get a lot shorter. Any restaurant with lit candles, cellophane-thin stemware, or salt served in a little open bowl should be immediately X-ed out. And not just because of all that disaster-inviting material preset on the table, but also because the clientele of such restaurants are generally not appreciative of spontaneous top-of-the-lungs shouts for "MORE JUICE!"

While I normally take the stance that childless people need to suck it up and accept the existence of babies—as one dad said to me, "My kids are part of the package now; where I go, they go"—I offer an exception for restaurant patrons. People go to restaurants of a certain caliber, and are often willing to pay a higher price to do so, to partake not only of the establishment's food, but also its atmosphere. Imagine that you and your wife finally get out for a quiet dinner without your child and purposely choose a fancy restaurant to provide a few hours of escape from the quotidian chores of parenthood. The last thing you'd want to hear during that meal is a crying baby, the very thing you're seeking relief from. There are certain places that you just shouldn't take a baby (subtitled movies and non-"capade" theatrical performances being some of them), which is why it is so important to seek out establishments where you know young patrons are anticipated. One sure sign is a menu with drawings of anthropomorphic hot dogs.

Some people assume that any restaurant that has a high chair is fair game, but this is no guarantee that the place is suitable for children. If the response to your request for a high chair is, "Oh, *um,* yeah, I think we've got to have one around here somewhere," or if the high chair comes to your table coated in a thick layer of dust, this is not a place that is regularly serving families with young children. Due to their lack of experience with baby customers, the staff will likely pay less-than-exceptional attention to the specific needs of someone so young. They may, for instance, lay out a full place setting—including a steak knife—for your baby.

Even a restaurant that advertises itself as "kid-friendly" can turn out to be surprisingly unequipped for kids. As many dads noted to me, it seems like the more young customers a restaurant has, the fewer fully functional high chairs or booster seats will be available.

Oh, they'll *have* the seats, and a busboy will lug one over to your table, but when you attempt to secure your toddler in place so that he neither climbs up into your fettuccini or does a backflip out of the chair onto a passing waitress, you'll find that the plastic latch on the seatbelt has been bent, broken in half, or torn completely off. I don't know what the other kids who use these chairs are doing to them (and, frankly, the thought of a toddler who can rip through a nylon strap chills me to the core), but the resulting damage means you somehow have to knot what's left of the belt around your baby.

The high-chair strap problem is vexing, but can be solved by including a few safety pins along with the bibs, bottles, and distraction toys you'll be toting along anyway. The absence of changing tables in the restrooms presents a far greater logistical problem. It's bad enough when the place only has changing areas in the women's room (although, provided your wife is along for the trip, that particular slight against dads can have a plus side for you), but when neither bathroom has one, an activity as simple as replacing your infant's soiled diaper can take on the mental and physical challenge of a *Fear Factor* stunt.

Changing a baby's diaper with one hand, while holding said child in midair with the other, is a feat I'd happily pay an admission fee to see; the simple fact of the matter is that you need to rest the kid on something. This is why many a man has jammed his legs up against the walls of a toilet stall to transform his knees into a makeshift changing table. The situation can be even worse for the dad who goes to his neighborhood's "hip" family diner: The place might have funky artwork, sippy cups, and crayons for the kids, but the restrooms may be grimy enough to turn you into a Howard Hughes–level germophobe.

And yet we still frequent such eateries with our children. We do so because, as a parent, it's easy to overlook pretty much every flaw if the restaurant serves food your child is willing to eat. Some little ones are picky from the get-go, but many of those who seem to be born lapping up whatever kind of esoteric dishes you plop down in front of them will reach an age at which they edit their once-eclectic menu down to about five foods (four of them starches). This culinary cut-off can be exceptionally hard on foodie dads—the kind of guys who prefer menus with glossaries. If you fall into this group, it's easy to get cocky when your new-to-solids infant is feasting upon paprika-dusted hummus, eggplant ragout, and chipotle polenta. But, the more you strut around singing the "my child eats everything" tune, the harder the fall that may await you. Somewhere around your kid's second birthday, she may inexplicably develop very picky taste buds, suddenly espousing new dietary edicts such as: "It must be breaded to be eaten." Some preschoolers won't touch food that can't be dipped in something. Others demand only colorless edibles. You can see why you might want to become a regular at whatever restaurant your child deems worthy.

Another major benefit to dining at an eatery swarming with kids is that your child's ruckus will be drowned out by the noise of the others. And if you think, "Oh, I don't need to worry about that, my baby is fine in restaurants," just wait. A lot of first-time dads are surprised by how much their child's public behavior can change between birth and age three. Infants are far easier to take out on the town than two- or three-year-olds. Newborns lie in their carriers, thoroughly amused by the sight of ceiling fans or the clinking of flatware, causing no more disturbance during a meal than the bread basket. Toddlers will want to taste—or at least feel—your food. When they can walk, they will want to leave their seats. When they can talk, they will tell you they don't like the color of the chairs, ask the people at the next table for a bite of their dinner, and break out into spontaneous verses of "Baa Baa Black Sheep" at Ethel Merman volume.

Oh, what swelled heads my wife and I got. Every time we'd take our perfectly behaved infant out to eat, we'd whisper to each other about what the parents at other tables might be doing wrong to wind up with a two-year-old who kept fleeing from his chair to do an airplane run around neighboring patrons. Only about a year and a half later, we got our comeuppance when we dined with another couple whose three-month-old happily snoozed through the meal, while Bryn tossed her utensils to the floor and shouted, "Fork down! Fork down!" like a battlefield medic.

With all honesty, I can say that while Bryn still keeps us on our toes during restaurant visits, she is a child who handles eating outside the home exceptionally well. We're lucky in that respect. I know plenty of great parents whose kids' restaurant behavior is not representative of their overall temperament. Perhaps it's overstimulation, or the fact that toddlers don't understand the concept of waiting to be served ("You can't expect a two-year-old to sit still for twenty minutes and not be disappointed when he sees that the food finally coming out is just the salad," said Christopher C. of Southington, Connecticut), but lots of children seem to lose their minds in restaurants. Should the worst-case scenario come to be, and your child causes a scene, "remove the kid from the premises for the sake of everyone else at the restaurant," advises Eric H. from Virginia. "If it happens, I take mine outside for a time-out; we'll walk around a bit, let him cool his heels, and go back inside when we're able."

Of course, there are some who don't want to sully their own dining experience by ducking outside with their kid. "That's why we don't eat anywhere fancier than Applebee's," Eric H. added. "I don't want to spend a lot of money on a meal I won't enjoy, either. The better restaurants are for dates with my wife."

It is when you dine out without the baby that you may suddenly become aware of the ways in which parenthood has changed your eating style. During the infancy, when your meals regularly have time to sit and congeal while the baby is fed, you may develop an acquired taste for food at room temperature. I heard from dads who had grown so accustomed to tepid meals that on the rare occasions that they got to sink their teeth into fresh-from-the-oven fare, it felt oddly foreign in their mouths.

Later on in the toddler years, when you're on constant guard for pasta-flinging and applesauce-splashing, you may be shocked to discover how rapidly you've learned to eat. A desire to deflect any meat-cube projectiles will often outweigh any desire to savor—or perhaps even chew—your own food. This leads to shovel-and-swallow eating. You may not even notice how quickly you devour your food until you're finally dining among other adults and you gulp down the last bite of your meal only to look around to notice others at the table still unfolding their napkins.

DINNER *AND* A MOVIE?

When your baby is very young, taking her into a theater to see a children's movie is pointless, unless maybe the film in question is the latest Pixar release and you want to see it yourself. Other than that, movie theaters are pretty much out for infants. Groups like Reel Moms have sprouted up in some cities around the country and present special "bring your babies" showings of current releases, the idea behind them being that if everyone in the crowd is holding an

---

A PROMISE UNKEPT: CHILDREN'S MENUS

You'll notice that most kids' menus have some kind of disclaimer like "For Children Under 11." That's because the meals are all sized for the most ravenous fifth-grader who might order them. If you order one for your toddler, you're likely to pay only slightly less than you would for an adult entrée and receive a serving of chicken fingers and fries that would take your little one a week to finish. Normally you could take home leftovers, but most kids' menu items are not the kind of food that keeps very well (reheated cheese sticks, anyone?).

If you're past the point of bringing your own jars of strained green beans to feed your baby at the restaurant, consider sharing your dinner with the kid. Or if you're not the sharing type, order him a side dish from the main menu. It will probably be cheaper, and it will give your toddler less ammunition for a postprandial food fight.

---

infant, nobody will complain when one starts crying. It's a great concept, but as you might guess from the group's name, not always the most enticing choice for dads. Fathers are welcome, but rarely go; and the selected films often fall cleanly within chick-flick parameters.

"I was craving a movie, and this friend of mine told me to try the next Reel Moms event," said one Southwestern dad. "I was all set to go until I read the listing and saw that they were screening that new Jennifer Lopez movie. That pretty much killed the idea for me."

By the time your child is a few years old, you'll be counting the days until the next Disney release. For many guys, including me, getting the full theater-going experience is worth sitting through a piece of animated claptrap that might not be at the top of your viewing list. In all truth, as an adult, you stand a much better chance of liking kiddie films today than back when, say, *The Care Bears Movie* was a big box-office draw. Just like children's music today, kids' movies are aiming to entertain both the young and the old in the audience. Disney's in-joke-laden *Aladdin* really started the trend in 1992, but *Shrek* was the film that took the "Make sure the grown-ups like it, too" mission to new heights.

The upside of this is that you get to see a truly great film like *The Incredibles;* the downside is that since it's really a grown-up movie that just happens to be animated, the violence may frighten your kids and the sophisticated humor could bore them.

"No one's making movies for kids anymore," said John S. of Cleveland. "PG is the new G."

Before you pull out five bucks for a child-sized popcorn, check out a Web site like ParentCenter.com that specifically reviews movies with a kid's-eye perspective. Or try doing what John S. does: Read the storybook adaptation of the movie to your child first (believe me, they won't be hard to find—and this is the only thing they're good for). "Once my son knows the plot," he said, "he can watch the movie without having to worry about what's going to happen to the characters. When a kid is already aware that the Omnidroid is not going to defeat Mr. Incredible, that scene is a lot less scary."

With a little help from Dad, toddlers might even be able to watch a film as devastating as *Bambi* without needing regression therapy in the future. "It's important for kids to be exposed to things they don't understand, things that can be scary or ambiguous, because it forces them to think for themselves," said Sachin W. of Chicago. "The effect is all dependent on your interaction, on the filtering that the parents do."

HAVE BABY—WILL TRAVEL

There's a major misconception among new parents that they won't be able to go away or take real vacations until a few years after the baby is born. In reality, it's quite the opposite. Infants are more easily transportable, especially if they nap their way through the majority of a long road trip or plane flight (though if they scream through the whole voyage, well, you have my pity). Toddlers are almost always more to handle: They require near constant stimulation.

When Bryn was five months old, my wife and I flew with her to a half-dozen different cities. All our friends thought we were crazy, but we proved them wrong; our daughter was flat-out wonderful on those trips. When she wasn't dozing, she was easily entertained by a little plush hippo or chewable dragonfly. Today, when we go on a flight with Bryn, not only do we have to pay for an extra ticket (most airlines insist that kids age two and up have their own seat), but we need to pack an endless supply of books and toys to occupy her—most of which she'll grow bored with before the plane leaves the runway. Then we're stuck relying on the in-flight magazine to make her happy for the remainder of the journey. Luckily, she's a big fan of the SkyMall catalog.

A few dads I spoke to have invested in portable DVD players for long plane flights. I think this is a brilliant idea. I can't imagine that even the most anti-TV person wouldn't be happier to have the toddler in the seat next to her watching a Barney video (with headphones, of course) rather than kicking her tray table and poking her with a chewy granola bar.

John P., a dad who lives in New York, frequently takes his two sons to see their grandparents in Australia. "We'll pack a huge pile of books, toys, DVDs, everything I can think of to keep them busy," he said. "And I also bring along earplugs and eye masks to offer to our neighbors on the plane."

On car trips at least you don't have to worry about annoying fellow passengers. But if your child's ability to occupy herself is in need of some honing, either you or your wife might have to play chauffeur, while the other sits in the back by the car seat (and if the baby's breast-feeding, it'll be you driving). That's a minor issue, though. A much bigger problem that occurs when you mix toddlers and automobiles is the frequency of potty stops.

"When we're in the car, sometimes I wish we'd never toilet trained him," said one Midwestern dad.

"Stopping to pee can turn a three-hour drive into a six-hour drive," said another.

Once your kid is diaper-free, you'll need to synchronize your own bathroom visits with hers. There's no way you're going to want to pull off into a rest stop one more time than necessary, even if that means driving with your legs crossed for fifty miles. And when your child does fall asleep on a long road trip, you and your wife may be so loathe to wake her up that the two of you drive along, staring at cornfields or silently counting blue cars rather than carrying on a conversation.

The moral of all this: Squeeze in as many trips as you can before your kid is able to ask, "Are we there yet?"

CHAPTER 19

Leisure Rehab

Nights out without a child in tow will occur about as frequently as requited crushes at *Babylon 5* conventions. It is important to make the most of these rare occasions. However, you must first relearn how to go out. Weeks or months of concentrated parenting may have provided you with the ability to find amusement in stacking a set of plastic rings, but your adult socialization skills may have atrophied in that time. On your first evening of child-free entertainment after the birth, you may feel like a modern-day Rip Van Winkle rediscovering the world around you.

Knowing that it may be a long time before the next kid-free evening, it's all too easy to waste your time worrying about whether you and your partner are doing an adequate amount of reveling. You might be tempted to try and squeeze too much into one night. Here's some advice: Don't try to cram dinner, a movie, drinks with friends, and a romantic moonlight stroll all into the four-hour stretch during which Grandma's watching the baby. Remember, you're out of practice—you don't want to pull something.

24 MINUTE PARTY PEOPLE: Too Much, Too Soon

A twist of career fate brought my wife and me to Minneapolis shortly before the birth of our daughter. With the majority of our friends back in New York, we were even more isolated than most couples in the first few months of parenthood. The sister of an old friend happened to live in the Twin Cities and so we received an invitation to a party that would be hosted and attended by people we'd never met before. The fact that we wouldn't know anybody there didn't deter us in the slightest; it had been months since we'd had a real social engagement and we were craving adult conversation. We got a sitter for the evening and zipped off to the party.

My wife and I definitely enjoyed ourselves that night, although we made a rather odd impression on the other guests. Like the shipwreck survivor who, after rescue from months on a deserted island, dives with feral gusto into whatever food his saviors pull from their pockets, we burst into that party with manic zeal. I bounded from person to person, introducing myself with a sudden inability to control either the volume of my voice or the speed of my speech.

I was taken aback by my own behavior; I had been looking forward to the party, sure, but certainly not vibrating with glee over the mere idea of it. But, when I opened the door and saw all those other grown-ups, something in me snapped and I was instantaneously transformed into a 1978 Robin Williams routine. (I think my wife was slightly more restrained.) With the natural high I was riding, I certainly wasn't in need of alcohol as a social lubricant, but it was a party, so I went and had a drink anyway.

This led to a shocking discovery on my part: The scant few opportunities I'd had for a beer or a glass of wine over the previous few months had not been enough to maintain my normal level of alcohol tolerance. After only two drinks I was already sensing a gravity-has-no-effect-on-me feeling. I ended up re-introducing myself to people whom I'd already been speaking to and constantly repeating my new catchphrase for the evening: "Hey, did I spill that?"

Thanks to the combination of premature inebriation and the rapid expenditure of energy, it took me little over an hour to burn out. I'd never gone from such a state of extreme hyperactivity to "Where can I lie down?" so quickly. After reconnecting with my equally exhausted wife, the two of us stepped onto the porch for a while to sober up, and then drove home (with her at the wheel), reminiscing the entire way about what a great hour we'd just had. When we got back to our place, our surprised sitter greeted us with, "Wow, you're home so early."

Our reply to her was truthful: "It's past our bedtime."

Based on other dads' tales, my story is pretty typical. A number of guys have said they got a little too giddy or a little too tipsy on their first night sans baby. So what are the lessons you can learn from my postnatal party experience? Let's discuss:

● **Go out—now!** The longer you wait, the more likely your first attempt at recreation will be a shock to your system. Yes, you need those first few months to grow accustomed to your new routines and responsibilities, but don't focus so much on learning the ropes that you lose track of your prefatherhood life completely. A few hours off here or there won't set you back so far that you become the dad from the JCPenney commercial. ("The first time my wife and I went out together without our daughter, I kept feeling like I was forgetting something; my hands were empty for the first time in two months," said Jeff R. from Chicago. "We felt like we were missing out on something important in the baby's life—whereas all we were missing out on was her sleeping.") Accept invitations whenever possible. And while dating your wife is important, so is getting out by yourself. Just alternate with your spouse so she can have some time away from family responsibility, too.

- **Understand your limitations**. It's not just alcohol tolerance that can go south after the baby arrives. One question I've heard from a lot of new dads is, "When do I find the time to exercise?" If the toughest workout you might get for a while is bench-pressing your infant, it follows that you may not be in peak physical condition. So, if you used to play in a weekend baseball league, don't expect to land any "Highlight of the Week" diving catches during your return game—at least not without ending up in traction.

- **Accept mediocrity.** When nights out with your wife are rare and require the services of a high-priced babysitter, you may insist that those evenings be nothing short of spectacular. I listened to countless dads complain about "the $70 movie"—and in some cities, it can honestly cost that much once you add the sitter's fee to ticket prices (visit the concession stand and you might as well cash out your 401k). You may find yourself saying, "This better be the greatest film I have ever seen in my life." And then, if you fail to be emotionally transported by what you normally might have considered a decent film, you consider the whole evening a bust. Grading a popcorn flick—or the food at a restaurant or the music at a concert—on the total monetary value of the event plus child care will make it near impossible to truly enjoy anything.

Remember that a two-star film is still two hours during which you didn't have to smell the antiseptic fragrance of a wet wipe.

- **Acknowledge the child.** Many men believe that to have a successful date with your wife, you need to leave the child at home, not only in the literal sense, but mentally as well. This is, of course, not going to happen—you *will* think about your kid. As will your spouse. So talk about the baby. Allow yourselves a good ten, fifteen minutes to mention how much you miss her, how you're wondering what she's doing at that moment, and how you can't wait to see her when you get home. Then you can drop the subject and go do something you can't do in front of the kid.

"The whole time I was out with my wife, I figured the kids were freaking out with the sitter. When we got home, I realized they'd never even noticed we were gone. I was like, 'Well, the least you could have done was miss me!'"

—George R., Austin, TX

TOO BUSY TO GET BUSY: Finding Sex Again

So many people say parenthood kills a sex life, but with all the new obstacles it presents, you'd think it should be just the thing for bringing a sense of excitement and adventure back into the mix. You'd *think* that.

Of all the pastimes you're eager to jump back into after the birth, sex is likely to top the list. Unfortunately, having it may become even more difficult than it was during the pregnancy. At least you didn't have to worry about waking the baby while it was still in the

---

GOOD TIMES IN SMALL PACKAGES

Pressure to make the most of every free moment can extend to nights at home, too. Once the baby is asleep, you may feel an imperative to take advantage of the peace, to do something constructive or exciting or romantic. But often, you will be too fatigued to do anything more strenuous than reach for a remote ("The free time you find is generally the time you're least interested in using for leisure activities," said John P. from New York City).

Too many parents look upon renting a DVD as giving up; they think of it as admitting the evening is a failure and just trying to kill time until tomorrow. This pessimism comes from the fact that most people think of movies and television as passive entertainment, but the smart guys out there know that the best part of watching a show or a film is talking about it afterward—deconstructing the good, ragging on the bad. Not to be too trite, but your couple time is precious. Renting *The Day After Tomorrow* is not a wasted evening; renting it and not making fun of it is.

"As soon as our son is asleep, we turn on the TV. It's the only thing we have energy for. Thank goodness for Netflix." —Jeffrey F., New York, NY

---

womb. When your kid is dozing in the next room, you and your wife will have to learn how to have incredibly quiet sex. For some, the added element of danger can be a turn-on, but for others, the possibility of their sweet, innocent child catching an errant grunt or groan is not exactly conducive to arousal. And, in the toddler years, you certainly don't want any surprise visitors: "Having my little girl burst in on us while Daddy is 'attacking' Mommy—that's a big concern," said Chad N. from Texas.

One certainty is that sex will not start up again right after the birth; expect a hiatus of several months. Most obstetricians will insist that nothing happens below the belt for at least six weeks, with the difficulty of the delivery and length of the recovery period possibly extending that time frame (it's generally longer if there was a cesarean section or an episiotomy). Even after intercourse gets a medical go-ahead, your wife may still be too sore or exhausted to really get in the mood. And realistically, in the beginning you might be so bone-tired yourself that just the thought of moving your hips makes you opt for a catnap over some nookie.

In time, hormones will take over for both of you and get things rolling again on the sex front. After what may have been a long period of unintentional abstinence, it may be somewhat slow-going at first. This is where sex as a parent takes you back to your teenage years: fumbling with a bra strap, bumping noses while going in for a kiss. It might take a little longer to find that spot on your wife's back where she really likes to be touched, but, hey, at least you remember that there is a spot.

> "After spending so much time with my daughter, when I'm alone with my wife, it can feel like she's a giant. I get so used to holding small hands and a tiny body, that holding my wife's hands feels awkward." —Rick D., San Francisco, CA

So assuming you'll find your way past the "How do I do this again?" feeling, the other big question is, "When?" The nap time quickie is very popular. And in a variation that I, myself, am not daring enough to try, some guys admit to popping a Disney video into the VCR and ducking into the next room—an hour of pleasure for everyone in the family. Some folks plan specific sexual liaisons. "Setting a standing appointment is especially important for me," said one Boston dad, "because my wife works really long days. I set up a two-hour babysitting session yesterday afternoon. I brought the little guy over to a neighbor's house, then went back to my house and made love with my wife. It was great."

There is one caveat to the pay-for-play idea: It only works if you can really afford it. Otherwise, you might put too much pressure on the experience to truly take pleasure in it; if you think forking over gobs of money to a babysitter places unduly high expectations on the quality of a movie you're going to see, imagine how it will make you rate the sex. It simply cannot help a relationship to follow up a lovemaking session with, "Well, that wasn't worth fifty bucks."

Plus, no matter how well you set the scene, the sex just might not happen. True story: My wife and I planned the ultimate romantic evening. We got dinner reservations at a favorite restaurant, a room at a highbrow hotel, and our very first overnight babysitter to cover things at home. After the fancy meal, we checked ourselves into our even-fancier room, and spent the remainder of the night in bed— with food poisoning.

So, the most common time for intimacy still seems to be night-time, after the kid is sleeping. The fatigue factor will always be there to contend with, but for most men, if there's one thing they can muster up that last ounce of energy for, it's the chance for an orgasm.

EPILOGUE

Remember the Time When the Baby Did That Thing?

One of the clichés that people routinely spout off when they want to sound like they have something deep to say about parenting is: "You have to make the most of the early years, because they'll be over before you know it." At some point, someone will say this to you while you've got a screaming baby balanced in one hand and an unidentified gooey substance dripping through the fingers of the other—and you will not believe this person. While you are living through your child's infancy, it may feel like it will never end; your baby will never sleep through the night, never stop throwing up on you, never simply ask you for a drink rather than bursting into tears anytime she wants one.

Of course, in a matter of months those little vexations *will* begin to fade away. And later, when your child is toddling around, giving you her opinions on subjects like puppies and apple juice, you don't want a swirl of dirty bibs and crying fits to be your overriding memory of her early days. This is why we work so hard to remember the good stuff. I have apparently not worked hard enough at this.

My friends and relatives constantly berate me for a dearth of Bryn pictures. And I admit, the camcorder and digital camera we bought during my wife's pregnancy are sorely underused. We've probably got an average of two hours' worth of footage for each year of her life so far, which makes for quite the gap-filled chronology ("Look, there's the baby when she first learned to sit up by herself! Oh, and now she's dancing around, singing 'Pop Goes the Weasel.'") The "memory book" we got as a shower gift is also about 80 percent blank, so I hope no one ever needs to know when she got her first haircut. I can't say I'll be surprised if someday Bryn is frustrated by how poorly we annotated her infancy.

At the risk of justifying my own disorganization, I contend that there's something to be said for putting the lens cap back on every once in a while. With streaming video and Internet photo-sharing, no one in the world has to miss out on your child's first unsuccessful attempt at riding a tricycle; however, you don't want to be so busy saving your baby's childhood for posterity that you're not 100 percent present while it's happening. Soon, your kid will start thinking of you as someone akin to a reality show cameraman, always hovering in the background ("Just act naturally; pretend I'm not here"). On one of the rare occasions that I *was* using my video camera, I was taping an impromptu dance performance Bryn decided to stage in our living room; after a while, she stopped bouncing and said, "Daddy, stop looking through that thing and watch me."

Believe me, we have pictures of Bryn—if she ever needs enough snapshots to illustrate her youth for an A&E *Biography* someday, the photos will be there. But my wife and I have focused more on remembering the things our daughter says, the random one-liners and baby bon mots that capture her personality at this young age. And, instead of relying on oral history to keep those anecdotes alive, we bought a little $1 notebook in which to write them down.

Without that spiral pad that sits on our mantle, I might have forgotten that when Bryn was two, she once said, "I got my blanket, I got my cup—that's happiness." Or that she reacted angrily to the ending of *Snow White and the Seven Dwarfs* by yelling, "I don't like the prince. Snow White should live with dwarfs or live by herself!" Or that she once made me blush when we passed by a Little League game and she started yelling, "Oh, boys! Hey, boys! Stop playing baseball and come look at me!"

And that notebook will someday be more than just a great keep-sake. When I eventually share the stories in it with Bryn's future friends and romantic partners, I will be fulfilling perhaps one of the most sacrosanct of fatherly duties: embarrassing my child.

ACKNOWLEDGMENTS

I owe a tremendous debt of gratitude to all the men—the vast majority of whom were strangers to me—who shared their thoughts and experiences, forwarded articles, recommended books and organizations, and referred me to even more dads: Tom Adair, Tavis Allison, Michael Aragon, Andrew Boardman, Joram Borenstein, Jason Boutin, Brian Boye, Mark Bradbourne, Brian Bradford, Bill Brown, Andrew Bub, Pete Cenedella, Ed Cerbone, Bradley Charbonneau, Jay Charness, Brett Cohen, Marc Cohen, Stuart Cohn, Patrick Colcernian, Christopher Coonce-Ewing, Rick Danielson, Ryan Deschamps, Rick Dodge, Daniel Eccher, Alex Elinson, Paul Engelhardt, Dave Falls, Jeffrey Felmus, Chris Ford, Robert Fraser, Shannon Frye, Ted Haegele, Eric Helm, Jeff Howe, Andrew Hughes, Ethan Hurd, Timi Johnstone, Michael Jordan, Larry Kanter, Jason Kauflin, James Kentner, Kevin Klein, Josh Levine, David Lewis, Michael Lorence, Jason Martin, Tom Mayer, Ted McCann, Cliff McIntosh, Jeff Middents, Scott Morgan, Doug Mouat, Chris Napierala, Chad Nusbaum, Alex Soojung-Kim Pang, Christopher Pepper, John Philp, Peter Reitzfeld, Bob Rice, Keith Richardson, Steve Royster, Jeff Ruby, George Rust, Eric Scott, Eric Seddon, Leonard Shostak, Joe Sliman, Mark Smithivas, Casey Spencer, Billy Sponseller, Richard Staviss, Herb Stephens, John Storhm, Jerry Tapp, Bill Templeton, Bill Tipper,

Nick Tucker, Bob Usdin, Read Vanderbilt, Sachin Waikar, Christopher Walker, Dave Weiss, Michael Whitt, Richard Wicker, Ramon Williamson, Joe Wills, Karl Wingren, Lee Winkelman, and Stuart Zang, as well as those who asked to remain anonymous.

Big thanks also need to go to Chris Howey for her thoughtful insights into my first draft, Lori Leibovich to whom I will be forever grateful for giving my career the boost it needed and assigning me the essays that gave seed to this book, and Gayle Forman for first saying to me, "You should write a book for dads."

Thanks to my wonderful agent, Jill Grinberg, for being ever-supportive and always tenacious in just the way you'd want an agent to be. Working with her has been nothing but a pleasure. And to David Cashion, my editor at Penguin, not only for believing in this book and shepherding me so gracefully through the revision process, but for being such a funny, cool, laid-back guy—which is exactly the kind of person I needed to deal with to keep my mind off just how difficult this project was. For a non-dad, he's also remarkably knowledgeable about the topic.

And I can go no further without profusely thanking my wife, Noelle Howey, for moral, creative, and grammatical support. She spent more than a few weekends going solo with our daughter so I could finish the book, and probably an equal amount of time reading over my rough drafts and being my first line of literary defense. She constantly pushed me to be a better writer (she's a brilliant author herself, so I lucked out there). And her keen eye for language saved these pages from an even greater proliferation of awful puns than what we ended up with (thanks to her, you didn't have to read the "paté/par-tay" line).

Finally, there's one person without whom this book would certainly never have existed: my daughter, Bryn. Without her, I literally would have had no material.

FOR THE BEST IN PAPERBACKS, LOOK FOR THE

In every corner of the world, on every subject under the sun, Penguin represents quality and variety—the very best in publishing today.

For complete information about books available from Penguin—including Penguin Classics, Penguin Compass, and Puffins—and how to order them, write to us at the appropriate address below. Please note that for copyright reasons the selection of books varies from country to country.

In the United States: Please write to *Penguin Group (USA), P.O. Box 12289 Dept. B, Newark, New Jersey 07101-5289* or call 1-800-788-6262.

In the United Kingdom: Please write to *Dept. EP, Penguin Books Ltd, Bath Road, Harmondsworth, West Drayton, Middlesex UB7 0DA.*

In Canada: Please write to *Penguin Books Canada Ltd, 90 Eglinton Avenue East, Suite 700, Toronto, Ontario M4P 2Y3.*

In Australia: Please write to *Penguin Books Australia Ltd, P.O. Box 257, Ringwood, Victoria 3134.*

In New Zealand: Please write to *Penguin Books (NZ) Ltd, Private Bag 102902, North Shore Mail Centre, Auckland 10.*

In India: Please write to *Penguin Books India Pvt Ltd, 11 Panchsheel Shopping Centre, Panchsheel Park, New Delhi 110 017.*

In the Netherlands: Please write to *Penguin Books Netherlands bv, Postbus 3507, NL-1001 AH Amsterdam.*

In Germany: Please write to *Penguin Books Deutschland GmbH, Metzlerstrasse 26, 60594 Frankfurt am Main.*

In Spain: Please write to *Penguin Books S. A., Bravo Murillo 19, 1° B, 28015 Madrid.*

In Italy: Please write to *Penguin Italia s.r.l., Via Benedetto Croce 2, 20094 Corsico, Milano.*

In France: Please write to *Penguin France, Le Carré Wilson, 62 rue Benjamin Baillaud, 31500 Toulouse.*

In Japan: Please write to *Penguin Books Japan Ltd, Kaneko Building, 2-3-25 Koraku, Bunkyo-Ku, Tokyo 112.*

In South Africa: Please write to *Penguin Books South Africa (Pty) Ltd, Private Bag X14, Parkview, 2122 Johannesburg.*